TEXTILES PRINTROOM. ART & DESIGN

The Anstey Weston
Guide to textile terms

The Anstey Weston

Guide to textile terms

Weston Publishing Limited

The Anstey Weston Guide to textile terms

Published by **Weston Publishing Limited**

First edition 1997

ISBN 0 9530130 0 6

Designed by John Miles
Printed and bound in England by Butler & Tanner Limited

Contents

for Anne Jill Lynn and Bella
Freddie and Toby

Foreword

This guide is intended for all who need accessible, up-to-date information about textiles. One group of readers will be those involved in textile manufacture; another, those whose studies include the use of textile materials. But there are many others, working perhaps in retailing or in a diversity of industries, whose primary training is not in textiles but whose work brings them into contact with textile products. This book is for them too.

Like all specialisms, textiles has evolved its own vocabulary to permit concise, accurate expression. This has been achieved in part by coining new words, and in part by taking words from ordinary language and investing them with particular, precise meanings. Without guidance, misunderstandings can arise over meanings, and costly mistakes can occur. There are particular dangers with textile terms that have been absorbed into ordinary language as metaphors, and whose meaning there has developed subsequently in a different way. The use of this guide can avoid such misunderstandings and prevent mistakes. It is a notable contribution to the explanatory literature of textiles.

Michael Woodhouse

Acknowledgements

The authors wish to acknowledge and thank the following for their contribution to this book.

Dr Keith Silkstone, Technical Executive at Marks & Spencer, for acting as editor, and for providing unfailing support and encouragement.
Dr Michael Woodhouse, Department of Textile Industries, University of Leeds, for writing the Foreword, and for reading the manuscript and offering many useful comments.
Peter Hetherington, Specialist Manager at Marks & Spencer, for advice on the Appendix.
John Lauder and Brian Hazell, Austicks University Bookshop, for invaluable advice on publishing and distribution.
Bob Franck and Paul Daniels of The Textile Institute, for comments on early and final drafts.
Nikky Nieburg, for proof-reading the manuscript.
Vera Whitehead, Librarian, Clothworkers Library, University of Leeds, and Jack Smirfitt, Editor of Textiles, for advice on sources.
Library staff at the College of Printing and Distributive Trades, Davies Street, London.
Mr A Krieger, BISFA, for supplying information for the Appendix.
The Textile Institute, for permission to use copyright material.

Eric and Della Alim, Bill Belcher, Kevin Byrne, Malcolm Cocks, Mark DH, Colleen Farr, Peter Gluckstein, Ruth Harris, Michael Harvey, David Hogan, Joanne Jatz, Catherine Moriarty, Jane Rapley, Gavin Rumble, Sofie Sutherland and Paul Tutton, for their varied and valued contributions.

Authors' note

This book is designed to be an easy-to-use, accessible introduction to textile terminology for students and those involved professionally in the fashion, textile and related retail industries. Our particular concern was to provide concise accurate information, in a format that allows easy exploration of the terminology for any specific topic.

The scope of a book of this size is necessarily limited: for further information the reader is referred to Textile Terms and Definitions, published by The Textile Institute, which has provided a constant reference for this publication, and to other specialist textile textbooks.

Helen Anstey and *Terry Weston*
May 1997

Helen Anstey is a graduate of the University of Leeds in textiles, and is currently Senior Lecturer in textile technology at the London College of Fashion. For many years she has lectured on training courses and worked as a consultant for major retail clothing companies.

Terry Weston is a graduate of the University of Leeds in textiles, and has lectured at both the London College of Fashion and the Central School of Art and Design. She is currently involved in a number of textile-related projects.

Guide to textile terms

How to use this guide

Index   All the technical terms and textile names in this textile guide are listed alphabetically in the index at the beginning of the guide.

References   Beside each index entry you will find one or more references: eg. A4 F.

These refer you to the particular section or sections of the guide where the entry is explained.

Each page where definitions appear is marked with the section reference in the top outer corner.

Sections   In each section the entries are listed in alphabetical order.

Sections of the guide	code

Fibres

General terms relating to fibres	**A1**
Generic names and associated terms	**A2**
Terms relating to fibre properties	**A3**
Miscellaneous terms relating to specific natural fibres	**A4**

Yarns

General terms relating to yarns	**B1**
Terms relating to yarn manufacture	**B2**
Yarn names	**B3**

Fabrics

General terms relating to fabrics	**C1**
Terms relating to weaving	**C2**
Terms relating to knitting	**C3**
Woven and knitted fabrics	**C4**
Terms relating to methods of fabric construction other than weaving and knitting, and fabrics made by these methods	**C5**

Dyeing	**D**
Printing	**P**
Finishing	**F**

Index

Notes to the index

1   **Terms that are defined in more than one section.**
Where the definition is substantially the same, reference
to the appropriate sections is made on the same line
eg.   pigment D P

Where the definition is substantially different, the entry
occurs more than once
eg.   shearing A4
     shearing F

2   **Certain terms are used interchangeably.**
The alternative term is introduced when the first term is
defined

   eg.   man made and **manufactured**
   eg.   brand name and **trade name**

cutting F
cuttling F

d

damage from sunlight A3
damask C4
decatising F
decitex B1
deep-dye D
deep-dyeing fibres D
degradation A3
degrade A3
degumming A4
delaine C4
delustrant A3
denier B1
denim C4
dent C2
desizing F
detergent F
devoré P
devoré print P
devourant print P
differential dyeing fibres D
dimensional stability A3 F
direct count B1
direct dye D
direct style P
discharge style P
discharge-resist process P
discharging agent P
disperse dye D
distressed F
dobby C2

doctor blade P
doeskin C4
dogstooth check C4
Donegal tweed C4
dope D
dope-dyed D
double atlas C4
double cloth C4
double jersey C4
double piqué C4
doubled B1
double-ended needle C3
doupion A4
drafting B2
drape A3 C1
drawing B2
dress-face finish F
drill C4
drip-dry A3 F
dry finish F
dry spun A1
dull A3
dupion A4
duplex printing P
durability A3
durable F
durable press F
dye D
dyebath D
dyed style P
dyeing D
dye-lot D
dyestuff D
dye-variant fibres D

e

easy-care A3 F
effect side C3
effect yarn B1
Egyptian cotton A4
eight-lock C4
elastane A2
elasticity A3
elastodiene A2
elastomer A1
elastomeric yarn B3
embossed crêpe F
embossing F
embossing calender F
emerizing F
ends C2
engraved P
engraved roller P
enzyme A3 F
exhaustion D
extensibility A3
extra dull A3
extra-warp fabric C4
extra-weft fabric C4
extrusion A1

f

fabric C1
fabric fault C1
fabric-dyed D
façonné C4
fading D
fall-on P

fancy yarn B1
fashioned / fully fashioned C3
fast D
fastness D
FBA F
fell C2
fellmongering A4
felt C5
felting shrinkage A3 F
fent C1
ferrous sulphate D
fibre A1
fibre cross section A3
fibre dyeing D
fibre length A3
fibre shape A3
fibre thickness A3
fibrillation B2
fibrillation F
fibroin A4
figure C1 P
filament A1
filament blend A3
filament blend yarn B3
filament yarn B1
finish F
finishing F
fire resistant F
fire retardant F
fixation P
flake yarn B3
flame resistance F
flame resistant F
flame retardant F
flammability A3 F

metallic print P
metallic yarn B3
metameric match D
metamerism D
microfibre A1
microporous polymer laminate C5 F
migration D P
milanese C4
Milano rib C4
mildew A3 F
mildew resistance A3
milling F
millitex B1
mineral fibre A1
minimum care A3
minimum iron A3
missed loop C3
missed stitch C3
mixing B2
mixture A3
mock leno C4
modacrylic A2
modal A2
modified cellulosic A1
mohair A2
mohair goat A2
moiré C4 F
moisture content A3
monofilament yarn B1
moquette C4
mordant D
mordant dye D
moss crêpe C4
moth damage A3 F

mothproof finish F
motif C1 P
mould / mold A3 F
mousseline C4
mull C4
multicolour print P
multifilament yarn B1
mungo A4
muslin C4

n

nap F
naphthol dye D
napping F
narrow fabric C1
natural dye D
natural fibre A1
natural polymer man made fibre A1
needle C3
needle bar C3
needle bed C3
needlebonded fabric C5
needled fabric C5
needlefelted fabric C5
needleloom C5
needlepunched fabric C5
nep B1
nepp yarn B3
net C5
net silk / nett silk A4
new wool A4
nip F
nip rollers D

piqué C4
piquette C4
pirn B2
plaid C4
plain C3
plain weave C2
plant fibre A1
plated fabric C3
plied B1
plissé C4
plush C4
polishing B1
polka rib C4
polyacrylonitrile A2
polyamide A2
polychromatic dyeing D
polyester A2
polyethylene A2
polymer A1
polymer resin F
polynosic A1
polyolefin A2
polypropylene A2
polytetrafluoroethylene A2
polyurethane A2
polyvinyl alcohol A2
polyvinyl chloride A2
polyvinyl derivatives A2
polyvinylidene chloride A2
ponte-Roma C4
poplin C4
post-cure F
potassium aluminium sulphate D
potassium dichromate D
power stretch B1

pre-cure F
pre-shrunk F
pressing F
Prince of Wales check C4
print paste P
printing P
printing styles P
proof F
protein fibre A1
PTFE A2
pulled wool A4
pulling (rag) A4
pulling (wool) A4
punto di Roma C4
pure new wool A4
pure silk A4
purl C3 C4
PVC A2

q

queenscord C4

r

race C2
raffia A2
rags A4
raising F
ramie A2
random dyeing D
raschel fabric C4
raschel machine C3
raw silk A4
reactive dye D

S

t

u

v

w

y

z

Fibres

A1 General terms relating to fibres

animal fibre: natural textile fibre from an animal, eg. silk, wool, cashmere, angora. Often called protein fibre.

bast fibre: natural textile fibre obtained from the stem or stalk of a plant, eg. linen, jute, ramie.

bicomponent fibre: man made fibre where more than one polymer for each filament is extruded through each hole in the spinneret.

brand name: name given by a textile company to their particular textile product, eg. Tencel (Courtaulds), Lycra (DuPont), Varuna (Liberty). Also known as trade name.

cellulosic fibre: natural textile fibre from a plant, eg. cotton, linen, sisal. The term is also used for man made fibres regenerated from plants, eg. viscose, modal.

continuous filament: a textile fibre of infinite length.

copolymer: a polymer in which the molecular repeating units are not all the same.

cotton wool: absorbent fibrous product made from cotton and/or viscose, used for medicinal and cosmetic purposes.

dry spun: describes man made filaments produced by dry spinning, where the dissolved polymer is converted into filaments by extrusion through the spinneret into warm air which causes the solvent to evaporate.

elastomer: any polymer with very high extensibility and substantially complete recovery.

extrusion: the process of forming filaments from fibre-forming substances by forcing them in plastic or molten form, or in solution, through the holes of the spinneret.

fibre: a long, thin, flexible solid structure, where the length is very much greater than the thickness.

filament: a textile fibre of infinite length.

fruit fibre: natural textile fibre from the fruit of a plant, eg. coir.

fur: the skin of certain animals with the hair on it, eg. fox fur, mink. A fur is not a textile because the fibres are still attached to the skin. If the fibres are removed from the skin they may be used as textile fibres, eg. wool can be obtained from sheepskin.

generic name: the name of the fibre. All textile fibres are classified: for natural fibres this relates to the fibre source, eg. cotton from the cotton plant, wool from sheep. For man made fibres the main basis for classification is the chemical structure, eg. poly*ester*, poly*amide*.

hair fibre: animal fibre other than sheep's wool and silk, eg. cashmere, mohair.

high wet modulus fibre: regenerated cellulose fibre with a wet strength very similar to that of cotton.

hollow fibre: a tube-like man made fibre or filament. Increases bulk and improves insulating properties.

leaf fibre: natural textile fibre from the leaf of a plant, eg. sisal, raffia.

man made fibre: a manufactured fibre, eg. viscose, polyester, as distinct from a fibre that occurs naturally.
See **manufactured fibre**.

manufactured fibre: alternative, and increasingly used, term for man made fibre.

melt spun: describes man made filaments produced by melt spinning, where the molten polymer is converted into filaments by extrusion through the spinneret into cold air which causes the polymer to solidify on cooling.

microfibre: extremely fine manufactured fibre or filament of 1 decitex or less (10,000 metres or 10 kilometres of filament weigh one gramme or less).

mineral fibre: natural textile fibre from a mineral, eg. asbestos.

modified cellulosic: manufactured fibre where the cellulosic raw material is chemically modified to produce a chemical derivative. Examples are cellulose acetate and cellulose triacetate.

natural fibre: a textile fibre occurring in nature which is animal, vegetable or mineral in origin.

natural polymer man made fibre: a fibre produced by man from naturally occurring polymeric substances where the physical form is changed, eg. viscose, a regenerated cellulosic fibre, is made from wood pulp from trees.

plant fibre: natural textile fibre from a plant, eg. cotton, linen.

polymer: a large molecule built up by the repetition of small, simple chemical units.

polynosic: regenerated cellulose fibre with a high wet modulus. These fibres are classified generically as modal fibres.

protein fibre: textile fibre from an animal, eg. wool, silk, mohair.

regenerated cellulosic fibre: man made fibre produced from plant material by chemical treatment which changes the physical form, eg. viscose from wood pulp from trees. NB. Regenerated cellulosic fibres are known as *rayon* in the USA and some other manufacturing countries. This term should strictly not be used in the UK.

regenerated fibre: man made fibre produced by treatment of a natural resource which changes the physical form but retains the chemical structure, eg. a regenerated protein fibre can be made from casein, a protein found in milk from the cow.

seed fibre: natural textile fibre from the seed of a plant, eg. cotton, kapok.

seed hair: fibre growing from the surface of a seed or from the inner surfaces of fruit cases or pods, eg. cotton.

speciality hairs: textile fibres grown from the skin of animals other than sheep, eg. mohair, cashmere, camel, angora, cashgora.

spinneret: metal plate perforated with holes through which the fibre-forming substances in either a plastic or molten state, or in solution, are extruded in man made fibre manufacture.

spinning solution: solution of fibre-forming polymer as prepared for extrusion through the spinneret.

staple fibre: a textile fibre of finite length, varying from 1.25 cms or 0.5 inches to 90 cms or 36 inches, depending on the fibre.

staple length: characteristic fibre length of a sample of staple fibres.

synthetic: describes a substance which has been manufactured by building up a complex structure from simpler chemical sustances.

synthetic fibre: *see* **synthetic polymer fibre**.

synthetic polymer fibre: man made textile fibre where the fibre-forming material is synthesised or built up from simpler chemicals, in contrast to fibres manufactured from naturally occurring fibre-forming polymers.

textile: term applied to fibres, filaments and yarns and the products made from them. Derived from the Latin *texere*: to weave.

trade name: name given by a textile company to their particular textile product, eg. Tencel (Courtaulds), Lycra (DuPont), Varuna (Liberty). Also known as brand name.

vegetable fibre: natural textile fibre from a plant.

wet spun: describes man made filaments produced by wet spinning, where the dissolved polymer is converted into filaments by extrusion through the spinneret into a coagulating bath of chemicals, causing the filaments to solidify.

A2

A2 Generic names and associated terms

acetate: man made natural polymer cellulose ester fibre. *Generic name.*

acrylic: man made synthetic polymer fibre. *Generic name.*

alpaca:
(1) natural animal hair fibre from the alpaca. *Generic name.*
(2) animal from which the fibre alpaca is obtained.

angora: natural animal hair fibre from the angora rabbit. *Generic name.*

angora goat: animal from which the fibre mohair is obtained. Also known as the mohair goat.

angora rabbit: animal from which the fibre angora is obtained.

aramid: man made synthetic polymer fibre. *Generic name.*

asbestos: natural mineral fibre. *Generic name.*

Bactrian camel: animal from which the fibre camel or camelhair is obtained.

camel: natural animal hair fibre from the Bactrian camel. *Generic name.*

camelhair: natural animal hair fibre from the Bactrian camel.

cashgora: natural animal hair fibre from the cashgora goat.

cashgora goat: animal from which the fibre cashgora is obtained.

cashmere: natural animal fibre from the cashmere goat. *Generic name.*

cashmere goat: animal from which the fibre cashmere is obtained.

china grass: alternative name for ramie, a natural vegetable bast fibre.

chlorofibre: man made synthetic polymer fibre. Both polyvinyl chloride and polyvinylidene chloride are classified as chlorofibres. *Generic name*.

coir: natural vegetable fruit fibre from the coconut. *Generic name*.

cotton: natural vegetable seed fibre from the cotton plant. *Generic name*.

cupro: man made natural polymer regenerated cellulosic fibre. *Generic name*.

elastane: man made synthetic polymer fibre with very high elasticity. *Generic name*.

elastodiene: man made natural or synthetic polymer fibre with very high elasticity. *Generic name*.

flax:
(1) alternative name for linen, a natural vegetable bast fibre. *Generic name*.
(2) plant from which the bast fibre linen or flax is obtained.

fluorofibre: man made synthetic polymer fibre. *Generic name*.

glass fibre: man made fibre obtained by drawing molten glass. *Generic name*.

guanaco:
(1) natural animal hair fibre from the guanaco. *Generic name*.
(2) animal from which the fibre guanaco is obtained.

hemp:
(1) natural vegetable bast fibre. *Generic name*.
(2) plant from which the bast fibre hemp is obtained.

horsehair: natural animal hair fibre from the mane and tail hair of horses and ponies. *Generic name*.

jute:
(1) natural vegetable bast fibre. *Generic name*.
(2) plant from which the bast fibre jute is obtained.

kapok: natural vegetable seed fibre from the kapok tree.
Generic name.

linen: natural vegetable bast fibre obtained from the flax
plant. *Generic name*.

llama:
(1) natural animal hair fibre from the llama. *Generic name*.
(2) animal from which the fibre llama is obtained.

lyocell: man made natural polymer regenerated cellulose fibre,
obtained by extruding cellulose dissolved in a recycleable
organic solvent.

metal fibre: man made fibre made from any metal. *Generic
name*.

modacrylic: man made synthetic polymer fibre. *Generic name*.

modal: man made natural polymer regenerated cellulose fibre.
Generic name.

mohair: natural animal hair fibre from the angora or mohair
goat. *Generic name*.

mohair goat: animal from which the fibre mohair is obtained.
Also known as the angora goat.

nylon: man made synthetic polymer fibre. Alternative name
for polyamide. *Generic name*.

pina: natural vegetable leaf fibre from the pineapple plant.
Also known as pineapple fibre.

polyacrylonitrile: man made synthetic polymer of which
acrylic fibres are largely composed.

polyamide: man made synthetic polymer fibre. Alternative
name for nylon. *Generic name*.

polyester: man made synthetic polymer fibre. *Generic name*.

polyethylene: man made synthetic polymer fibre. *Generic
name*.

polyolefin: man made synthetic polymer. Polypropylene and polyethylene are both polyolefin fibres.

polypropylene: man made synthetic polymer fibre. *Generic name.*

polytetrafluoroethylene: man made synthetic polymer fibre, also known as PTFE. It is a fluorofibre.

polyurethane: man made synthetic polymer fibre.

polyvinyl alcohol: man made synthetic polymer of which vinylal fibres are composed.

polyvinyl chloride: man made synthetic polymer, also known as PVC. It is a chlorofibre.

polyvinyl derivatives: group of man made synthetic polymer fibres, including the generic fibres acrylic, modacrylic, chlorofibre, vinylal and fluorofibre.

polyvinylidene chloride: man made synthetic polymer. It is a chlorofibre.

PTFE: abbreviation for polytetrafluoroethylene, a man made synthetic polymer. It is a fluorofibre.

PVC: alternative name for polyvinyl chloride, a man made synthetic polymer. It is a chlorofibre.

raffia: natural vegetable leaf fibre obtained from the raffia palm.

ramie:
(1) natural vegetable bast fibre. *Generic name.*
(2) plant from which the bast fibre ramie is obtained.

silk: natural animal protein fibre obtained from the cocoons produced by silkworms. *Generic name.*

sisal:
(1) natural vegetable leaf fibre. *Generic name.*
(2) plant from which the leaf fibre sisal is obtained.

triacetate: man made natural polymer cellulose ester fibre. *Generic name.*

vicuna:
(1) natural animal hair fibre from the vicuna. *Generic name*.
(2) animal from which the fibre vicuna is obtained.

vinylal: man made synthetic polymer fibre. *Generic name*.

viscose: man made natural polymer regenerated cellulose fibre. *Generic name*.

wool: natural animal fibre obtained from the fibrous covering of the sheep. *Generic name*.

A3 Fibres

A3 Terms relating to fibre properties

abrasion: wearing away by rubbing.

absorbency: ability of a fibre to take up moisture.

acid: compound of hydrogen in which the hydrogen can be replaced by a metal, or with a basic metallic oxide to form a salt of that metal and water.

alkali: compound of hydrogen and oxygen with sodium, potassium or other substances, which is soluble in water, and will react with an acid to form a salt and water.

biological attack: damage done to textiles by living plant and animal organisms, eg. cellulosic fibres are prone to attack by moulds and mildews, and wool fibres are prone to attack by the clothes moth.

bleach: chemical substance which will remove colour from textiles by either an oxidising or a reducing action.

bleaching: process of removing colour from textiles using a chemical substance called a bleach.

bleaching agent: a chemical reagent capable of destroying partly or completely the unwanted colour in textile materials, leaving them white or considerably lighter in colour.

blend: combination of two or more different staple fibres within the same yarn. Fibres are blended for one or more reasons, eg. cost, properties, appearance.

blending: process of efficiently combining different fibres together.

bright: term used to describe textile materials, especially man made fibres and yarns, where the lustre has not been significantly reduced.

bursting: rupture of a fabric under mechanical stress where the force is upwards and outwards as with the bending of knees and elbows. The bursting strength is partially dependent upon fibre strength.

carpet beetle: species of beetle, the larvae of which attack wool and the speciality hairs.

chemical attack: damage to textile fibres caused by chemicals, eg. acids damage cellulosic fibres, and wool is damaged by alkalis.

clear: refers to man made fibres which have not been delustred, and therefore have a glassy, highly lustrous appearance.

clothes moth: species of moth, the larvae of which attack wool and the speciality hairs.

crease-resistant: refers to the ability of a fabric to resist creasing and/or recover from creasing. Resilient fibres such as wool make good crease-resistant fabrics, while less resilient fibres such as cotton and linen give fabrics poor crease-resistant properties.

creasing: formation of unwanted folds and puckers in fabric during use, which adversely affect the appearance.

crimp: the waviness of a fibre, eg. wool fibres have a characteristic natural crimp. Man made fibres can be produced with crimp if required.

crocking: abrasive action on a textile to which dyes and pigments have a measurable fastness. Alternative name for rubbing.

damage from sunlight: certain fibres are weakened by exposure to strong or prolonged sunlight, eg. nylon becomes weaker and, if white, turns yellowish.

degradation: undesirable change in the properties of a textile, due to chemical and/or biological decomposition.

degrade: cause chemical and/or biological decomposition.

A3

delustrant: substance added to the spinning composition before extrusion in man made fibre manufacture in order to reduce the lustre of the man made fibre produced. The white pigment titanium dioxide is most commonly used.

dimensional stability: ability of a textile, as fibre, yarn, fabric or finished product, to retain its dimensions through processing and use.

drape: how a fabric hangs or falls and how it behaves when folded, pleated or gathered. Drape is affected by the properties of the fibre(s) in the fabric, yarn type, fabric structure, finish and weight.

drip-dry: describes fabrics where crease resistance is good during wear and washing, and minimum ironing is necessary to maintain a good appearance.

dull: lacking in lustre.

durability: ability of a textile to perform adequately for its expected time span.

easy-care: describes fabrics where crease resistance is good during wear and washing, and minimum ironing is necessary to maintain a good appearance.

elasticity: ability of a textile (fibre, yarn or fabric) to stretch and return to its original shape.

enzyme: one of a number of naturally occurring complex proteins that speeds up a specific biochemical reaction without itself being changed. It acts as a catalyst.

extensibility: ability of a fibre to stretch.

extra dull: describes a man made fibre or filament where the amount of delustrant is very high, and the fibre/filament appears opaque and without lustre.

felting shrinkage: shrinkage caused by the irreversible matting of wool and other animal hair fibres when subjected to heat, moisture and intermittent mechanical pressure. Caused largely by the overlapping scale structure on the surface of the fibre.

fibre cross section: characteristic appearance of a fibre when a cross section is viewed under a microscope.

fibre length: the distance between the two ends of the fibre.

fibre shape: the overall external form of the fibre.

fibre thickness: the average diameter of the fibre.

filament blend: man made blend where two or more different filaments are spun at the same time.

flammability: the ability of a textile to burn with a flame under specified test conditions.

fungi: plant forms which have no chlorophyll and derive nourishment from organic matter. Examples include moulds and mildews.

handle: how a textile feels when touched with the hand, eg. warm, rough, soft, smooth, cool.

heat setting: process where a thermoplastic fibre (as fibre, filament, yarn, fabric or garment) can be set into a permanent shape by applying heat under tension, followed by cooling whilst maintaining the tension.

hydrophobic: literally water-hating. Used to describe fibres that absorb little or no water, eg. polyester.

lustre: the sheen of a fibre. This is dependent on the amount of light that is reflected from the fibre. Fibres with a high degree of lustre can be described as bright.

man made filament blend: man made blend where two or more different filaments are spun at the same time.

matt: relatively dull with little or no lustre.

mildew: a growth of certain species of minute fungi, which flourish in damp, warm conditions, and which may cause stains on certain fabrics which are very difficult to remove.

mildew resistance: ability of a fibre to resist attack by mildew.

minimum care: describes fabrics where crease resistance is good during wear and washing, and minimum ironing is necessary to maintain a good appearance.

minimum iron: *see* **minimum care**.

mixture: fabric where more than one type of fibre is present but the fibres are not intimately blended within the yarn(s).

moisture content: a numerical percentage value expressing the ratio of the mass of moisture in a material to the total moist mass.

moth damage: damage inflicted on wool and other animal hair fibres by the larvae of the clothes moth.

mould / mold: a growth of certain species of minute fungi which flourish in damp, warm conditions, and which may cause stains on certain fabrics which are very difficult to remove.

non-flammable: not capable of burning with a flame under specified test conditions.

organic solvent: hydrocarbon substance capable of dissolving another substance.

permanent set: dimensional stability imposed on a textile (as fibre, yarn or fabric) where structural change ensures that the effect remains throughout the useful life of the product.

photodegradation: damage caused by the absorption of light and subsequent chemical reactions. Ultra-violet radiation is particularly damaging.

pilling: the entangling of fibres during washing, dry-cleaning or wear to form unsightly balls or pills, which stand up from the surface of the cloth.

pills: unsightly balls of fibre which stand up from the surface of the cloth.

regain: a numerical percentage value expressing the ratio of the mass of moisture in a material to the oven-dry mass.

resilience: ability of a fibre or fabric to spring back to its original shape after being crushed.

rot: decay caused by natural forces.

rot resistance: ability of a fibre to withstand decay caused by naturally occurring algae and/or fungi.

rubbing: abrasive action on a textile which can affect the appearance, through damage to the structure, and can affect the colour, if the colorant used is not resistant to rubbing.

scales: the fibre surface of wool and other animal hairs is covered with overlapping scales. This causes each fibre to move more easily in one direction than the other, and can cause felting, where the fibres become irreversibly matted and tangled.

semi-dull: term used to describe a man made fibre containing some delustrant which reduces the lustre to a level between bright and dull.

shrinkage: reduction in length and/or width of a textile as a result of treatments during processing or use.

shrink-resist: describes a textile material that is dimensionally stable.

solvent: substance capable of dissolving another substance.

static electricity: electricity produced by materials rubbing together. Can be a problem with synthetic fibres with low absorbency.

strength: ability of a textile, as fibre, yarn or fabric, to withstand physical stress.

stretch: term specifically used in the textile industry to describe a fabric or yarn with greater than usual extensibility and recovery.

super-dull: describes a man made fibre with a large amount of delustrant present so that the appearance is extremely matt.

tearing: laceration of a fabric, eg. by catching the sleeve of a shirt on a protruding nail and rending it. The resistance to tearing is partially dependent on fibre strength.

tendering: local deterioration in a fabric caused by adverse reaction between the dye or finish on the fabric and an agency such as light.

thermoplastic: capable of being set into a particular shape with heat. This fibre property allows textiles to be heat-set. If the shape is held while the textile cools down the textile will retain that shape provided that the temperature of heat setting is not approached again.

titanium dioxide: white pigment used to reduce the lustre of man made fibres, by adding it to the spinning composition before extrusion of the filaments.

trilobal: refers to the shape of particular synthetic polymer fibres and filaments where the cross section shows three rounded surfaces which scatter and reflect additional light, thereby increasing the lustre.

wash and wear: describes fabrics and garments where crease resistance is good during wear and washing, and minimum or no ironing is necessary to maintain a good appearance.

wear and tear: damage to a textile, as fibre, yarn, fabric or garment, through use. Weak fibres such as wool and viscose are less durable and hard wearing than strong fibres such as cotton and nylon.

white pigment: the white pigment titanium dioxide is used as a delustrant in man made fibre manufacture.

A4 Miscellaneous terms relating to specific natural fibres

COTTON

American cotton: type of cotton of medium fineness and medium staple length.

boll: the seedcase and its contents on the cotton plant.

Egyptian cotton: type of cotton characterised by long, fine fibres.

ginning: process that removes the cotton fibres (lint) from the seed.

Indian cotton: type of cotton characterised by relatively short, coarse fibres.

lint: the main seed hair of the cotton plant.

linters: whole and broken lint fibres and fuzz fibres, which are removed from the ginned cotton seed by a special ginning process.

Sea Island cotton: type of cotton with the longest and finest fibres.

LINEN

hackling: combing process used in the manufacture of linen yarn.

line flax: longer, combed flax fibres made into better quality linen yarns.

retting: chemical or biological treatment of flax stalks to make easier the separation of the fibre bundles from the woody part of the stem.

scutching: operation of separating the flax fibre from the woody part of the flax stem.

tow: shorter flax fibres removed by hackling and made into linen yarns.

SILK

bave: silk fibre as withdrawn from the cocoon formed by a silkworm. It consists of two filaments (brins) made of the protein fibroin, held together with the natural gum sericin which is also a protein.

boiling-off: removal of the natural gum or sericin from silk yarns or fabrics by treatment with a hot, mildly alkaline solution. Also known as degumming.

brin: single filament of silk resulting from the degumming of the bave withdrawn from the cocoon.

cocoon: egg-shaped casing of silk spun by the silkworm to protect itself as a chrysalis or pupa.

degumming: removal of the natural gum or sericin from silk yarns or fabrics by treatment with a hot, mildly alkaline solution. Also known as boiling-off.

doupion: silk-breeding term meaning double cocoon, used to describe the irregular, raw rough silk reeled from double cocoons.

dupion: *see* **doupion**.

fibroin: one of the proteins of which the silk fibre is composed. When the silk is degummed the sericin is removed, leaving the fibroin.

net silk / nett silk: yarn formed from continuous filament silk. Also used to describe fabrics made from net silk.

pure silk: silk in which there is no metallic or other weighting of any kind, except that which is an essential part of dyeing.

raw silk: continuous filaments containing no twist, drawn off or reeled from cocoons. The filaments are unbleached, undyed and not degummed.

reeling: process of unwinding the silk filaments from the cocoons.

scroop: rustling sound produced when a material with a particular handle is compressed by hand. It is generally associated with silk, but can be produced in certain cellulosic fabrics that have been given suitable finishing treatments.

sericin: protein in silk fibre cementing the two fibroin filaments (brins) in the bave.

silk noil: very short silk fibres extracted during silk combing that are too short for producing spun silk. These fibres are usually spun into silk-noil yarns.

spun silk: staple fibre silk yarn produced from silk waste which has been largely degummed.

throwing: formation of continuous filament silk yarns by twisting.

thrown silk: yarn twisted from continuous filament silk.

tussah: coarse silk produced by a wild silkworm, with characteristic irregularities along the filaments.

waste silk: fibres remaining after reeling and throwing, and silk from damaged and unreelable cocoons.

weighting: the addition of metallic salts to silk to increase the mass or weight and to impart a firmer handle.

wild silk: silk fibres from species other than Bombyx mori.

WOOL

botany wool: term for tops, yarns and fabrics made from wool from the merino sheep. The term originates from Botany Bay in Australia, where the first merino flocks brought to Australia were landed.

crossbred: type of medium fine, medium length wool grown by crossbred breeds of sheep.

fellmongering: the pulling of wool from the skins of dead sheep.

fleece wool: any wool shorn from a living sheep.

kemp: coarse fibres present in varying amounts in wool fleece. Usually white, black or brown and can be used to give decorative effects in some wool fabrics.

lambswool: wool from the fleeces of lambs (young sheep up to the stage of weaning).

merino wool: wool from the merino sheep, which produces the shortest and finest wool fibres.

mungo: fibrous material made in the woollen industry from pulling, or tearing up into fibres, new or old tightly woven or milled cloth or felt in rag form.

new wool: fibre from a sheep or lamb that has not previously been used. Alternative term for virgin wool.

pulled wool: wool that has been removed from the skins of dead sheep.

pulling (rag): the operation of reducing rags and thread waste to a fibrous state.

pulling (wool): removal of wool from the skins of dead sheep.

pure new wool: term used when all the wool present in a fabric is virgin wool.

rags: waste fabric from garment manufacturing and old, used garments. Rags are classified as new or old, depending on whether the material has been used or not.

recovered wool: wool rags and manufactured waste, torn up and reprocessed into fibres again, and used for producing shoddy and mungo yarns. Also known as recycled wool, remanufactured wool, reused wool.

recycled wool: *see* **recovered wool**.

remanufactured wool: *see* **recovered wool**.

reused wool: *see* **recovered wool**.

shearing: cutting the wool fleece from a live sheep.

Shetland wool: descriptive term for wool from the Shetland sheep originating in the Shetland Islands. It is generally qualified by one of the adjectives: pure, genuine, real, which implies that the wool actually originated in the Shetland Islands, rather than being merely a wool of similar characteristics.

shoddy: fibrous material made in the woollen industry from pulling knitted or loosely woven fabric in rag form, that may be new or old.

skin wool: wool removed from the skins of slaughtered sheep. The roots of the fibres are loosened by steeping in lime, or by the bacterial action caused by sweating, or by painting the flesh side with sodium sulphide.

slipe wool: skin wool obtained by steeping in lime.

virgin wool: fibre from a sheep or lamb that has not previously been used. Alternative term for new wool.

Yarns `B1`

B1 General terms relating to yarns

blended yarn: spun yarn containing two or more different fibres intimately combined, eg. cotton and polyester, wool and cashmere. The proportions of each fibre in the blend are specified.

bulk: refers to the volume of a yarn (how much space it takes up) related to its size or count (relationship between length and mass or weight). A bulky yarn occupies more space than a yarn of similar count that is not bulky.

cabled yarn: two or more folded yarns twisted together. One or more components in a cabled yarn can be a single yarn. Cabled yarns are also known as corded yarns.

carded: refers to yarns where the fibres have been disentangled, cleaned, mixed and partially straightened on a carding machine during yarn manufacture.

combed: refers to yarns where the fibres have been further disentangled after carding and before spinning. This removes short fibres and makes the remaining longer fibres lie more parallel, giving a stronger, finer, smoother and more lustrous yarn.

combed cotton: cotton yarns and fabrics where longer, better quality fibres have been combed after carding and before spinning. Combed cotton yarns and fabrics are more expensive because of the additional processing involved, and the better quality of the raw material.

comfort stretch: degree of elasticity within a yarn or fabric which ensures continuing good fit in garments which conform to the body, eg. tights, tube dresses, leggings.

continuous filament yarn: yarn made of one or more continuous strands called filaments where each component strand or filament runs the whole length of the yarn. Continuous filament yarns are

B1

also known as filament yarns, and fabrics made from them can be called filament fabrics.

corded yarn: two or more folded yarns twisted together. One or more components in a corded yarn can be a single yarn. Corded yarns are also known as cabled yarns.

cotton count: indirect count system used for cotton and other fibres spun on the cotton system. The count number is the number of hanks, each measuring a standard 840 yards, that weigh one pound. 30s cotton count means that 30 hanks, each of 840 yards, weigh one pound. 40s cotton count means that 40 hanks, each of 840 yards, weigh one pound.

count: numerical expression of the size of a yarn.

count system: a particular system used to express by number the size of a yarn. All count systems are based on the relationship between the length of a yarn and the mass or weight of the yarn. With indirect count systems the weight is fixed and the length is variable: a higher count number indicates a finer yarn. With direct count systems the length is fixed and the weight is variable: a higher count number indicates a thicker yarn.

covering power: ability of a yarn to take up space within a fabric, eg. a textured yarn will have greater covering power than the same yarn before texturing.

decitex: the mass or weight in grammes of 10,000 metres of a fibre, filament or yarn. It is also the mass or weight in decigrammes (0.1 gramme) of 1,000 metres or 1 kilometre of a fibre, filament or yarn. Used for very fine yarns and filaments, eg. microfibres.

denier: the mass or weight in grammes of 9,000 metres of a fibre, filament or yarn.

direct count: count system where the length is fixed and the mass or weight is variable: a higher count number indicates a thicker yarn. Examples of direct count systems include denier, tex and decitex.

doubled: refers to a yarn where two or more single yarns have been twisted together. Such yarns are known as folded, doubled or plied yarns.

effect yarn: name for fancy yarn in other European countries.

fancy yarn: yarn with deliberately produced irregularities in its construction. These irregularities are generally formed by varying the speeds at which one or more of the component yarns are delivered to the twisting machine, and fibres may be incorporated for particular types of fancy yarn. Fancy yarns are made from a variety of fibre types and are used for decorative effects in fabrics.

filament yarn: yarn made of one or more continuous strands called filaments where each component strand or filament runs the whole length of the yarn. Filament yarns are also known as continuous filament yarns, and fabrics made from them can be called filament fabrics.

folded: refers to a yarn where two or more single yarns have been twisted together, eg. 2-fold yarn, 3-fold yarn. Such yarns are known as folded, doubled or plied yarns.

gassed yarn: yarn that has been passed through a flame or over a heated element to remove unwanted surface fibres, to give a smoother surface.

hank: unsupported coil of yarn, where the two ends are tied to maintain the shape of the coil. Alternative name for skein.

hard twist: describes a yarn that has been given a greater than usual amount of twist.

high tenacity yarn: yarn made from fibres with greater than usual strength, generally used for industrial products such as tyre cords.

indirect count: count system where the mass or weight is fixed and the length is variable: a higher count number indicates a finer yarn. Examples of indirect count systems include cotton, worsted and Yorkshire woollen.

kilotex: the mass or weight in kilogrammes of 1 kilometre or 1,000 metres of yarn.

marl: two slubbings or rovings of different colour or lustre are run together and drafted into one. In the worsted industry the term has a very precise meaning, and a number of sub-divisions are found, eg. single marl, double marl, half-marl. More generally the term is used loosely to describe a yarn showing two distinct colours.

mélange: describes a yarn produced by mélange printing of slubbings, tops or slivers, where bands of colour are printed at intervals. *See* **mélange printing**.

millitex: the mass or weight in milligrammes of 1 kilometre or 1,000 metres of a fibre, filament or yarn.

monofilament yarn: yarn made up of one strand or filament which runs the whole length of the yarn.

multifilament yarn: yarn made up of a number of strands or filaments, each of which runs the whole length of the yarn.

nep: small knot of entangled fibres.

novelty yarn: name for fancy yarn in the United States.

opacity: degree of opaqueness; not translucent or transparent.

plied: refers to a yarn where two or more single yarns have been twisted together. Such yarns are known as folded, doubled or plied yarns.

polishing: process used on certain yarns, notably some sewing threads, to give a very smooth surface, thus reducing the friction between yarn and sewing machine. It involves sizing, drying and frictional treatment with burnishers.

power stretch: degree of elasticity within a yarn or fabric which enables it to be suitable for figure control garments used in corsetry.

roving: fine continuous length of staple fibres formed during preparation for the final spinning operation.

S twist: twist in yarn where the direction of the twist follows the direction of the central part of the letter 'S', ie. top left to bottom right.

sewing thread: a thread or yarn made for the purpose of machine or hand sewing. It must be strong, even, round, smooth and balanced in twist. Sewing threads may be spun, monofilament, multifilament, textured, corded or core-spun, and are often given special finishes to improve their properties.

single yarn / singles: yarn produced by one unit of the spinning machine.

skein: unsupported coil of yarn, where the two ends are tied to maintain the shape of the coil. Alternative name for hank.

sliver: loose open continuous length of staple fibres without twist formed during preparation for spinning.

slubbing: thick continuous length of staple fibres formed during preparation for spinning.

spun: used to describe a staple fibre yarn where the fibres are twisted together in order to form a continuous length.

spun yarn: *see* **staple fibre yarn**.

staple fibre yarn: yarn made from staple fibres which are twisted together in order to form a continuous length.

stretch yarn: yarn with greater than usual degree of stretch and recovery. Stretch yarns include some textured yarns and all elastomeric yarns.

tex: the mass or weight in grammes of 1 kilometre or 1,000 metres of a fibre, filament or yarn.

texture: the surface appearance and handle of a yarn or fabric.

textured yarn: man made filament yarn that has been treated by one of a variety of methods to introduce durable crimps, coils and loops along the length of the filaments.

top: combed sliver produced on the worsted spinning system.

tow: mass of man made filaments free from twist.

twist: the spiral formation given to fibres during spinning to ensure cohesion. The degree of twist in spun and filament yarns influences the character of the yarn.

B1

twist-lively: very highly twisted or hard twisted S or Z twist yarn that tends to snarl or twist around itself when free from tension.

woollen: refers to wool yarns spun on the woollen system, and to fabrics and garments made from woollen yarns. Woollen yarns are relatively hairy and less regular, because the short fibres are not removed by combing, and because the fibres do not go through so many processes before spinning.

worsted: refers to wool yarns spun on the worsted system, and to fabrics and garments made from worsted yarns. Worsted yarns are made from combed fibres, and the yarns are relatively strong, smooth, fine and lustrous.

worsted count: indirect count system used for worsted and other fibres spun on the worsted system. The count number is the number of hanks, each measuring a standard 560 yards, that weigh one pound. 60s worsted count means that 60 hanks, each of 560 yards, weigh one pound. 40s worsted count means that 40 hanks, each of 560 yards, weigh one pound.

yarn: a fine continuous length of fibres and/or filament(s), with or without twist, that is strong enough to be processed into fabric.

YSW (Woollen Yorkshire): indirect count system used for wool and other fibres spun on the woollen system. The count number is the number of skeins, each measuring a standard 256 yards, that weigh one pound. 30s YSW count means that 30 skeins, each of 256 yards, weigh one pound. 20s YSW count means that 20 skeins, each of 256 yards, weigh one pound.

Z twist: twist in yarn where the direction of the twist follows the direction of the central part of the letter 'Z', ie. top right to bottom left.

B2 Terms relating to yarn manufacture

blending: preparatory process in spinning which efficiently combines fibres, which may be different qualities or colours of the same generic fibre, or different generic fibres, to achieve an even distribution.

bobbin: cylindrical or slightly tapering former, with or without flanges, onto which slubbings, rovings, slivers or yarns are wound.

cake: cylindrical package of continuous filament viscose yarn.

card: alternative name for a carding machine.

carding: preparatory process in spinning, where staple fibres are disentangled, cleaned, mixed and partially straightened. The fibres leave the card either as a continuous web or as a continuous rope of fibres, and pass on to subsequent stages of preparation for spinning.

carding machine: machine used to disentangle, clean, mix and partially straighten staple fibres as a preparatory stage in spinning.

cheese:
(1) a cylindrical support on which yarn is wound.
(2) a cheese-like package of yarn wound on a cylindrical support.

cleaning: processes used to rid textiles, as fibre, yarn or fabric, of dirt and other unwanted matter. Various cleaning operations are undergone before fibres can be processed into yarn: the processes used depend on the fibre(s) being processed, and on the type of yarn that is being produced.

combing: preparatory process in spinning after carding where short fibres are removed and the remaining longer fibres are made to lie more parallel. The yarns made from combed fibres are stronger, finer, smoother and more lustrous than yarns made from fibres that have not been combed, and for these reasons are also more expensive.

cone:
(1) a conical support on which yarn is wound.
(2) a conical package of yarn wound on a conical support.

cop: term used to describe several different types or shapes of yarn package.

cotton system: spinning system developed specifically for cotton fibres, but which is now used in addition for other fibres and fibre blends where the fibres are of similar dimensions to cotton.

crush cutting: method of cutting continuous filament tow into staple fibres of predetermined length, where the filaments of the tow are severed by crushing between an anvil roller and a cutting roller with blades helically arranged around its circumference.

cutting: process where man made continuous filaments are cut into staple. Yarns made from these staple fibres are called spun yarns.

drafting: the process of progressively drawing out slivers, slubbings or rovings into finer strands. When the strands are sufficiently fine the final drafting takes place, twist is inserted and the spun yarn is produced.

drawing:
(1) preparatory stage in staple fibre spinning where the slivers are progressively reduced in diameter by drafting into slivers or rovings of suitable size for spinning.
(2) process of stretching man made filaments after extrusion under controlled tension. This orientates the molecules and increases the strength of the filaments.

fibrillation: process of stretching a film or sheet of plastic until it splits up into a network of interconnected fibres.

lap: sheet of fibres, formed at various intermediate stages in textile processing.

mixing: preparatory process in spinning where fibres are combined together to ensure an even distribution.

noil: the shorter fibres separated from the longer fibres by combing during a preparatory process before spinning.

oiled wool:
(1) unscoured or undyed knitting wool.
(2) wool dyed before spinning and containing added oil not subsequently removed.

opening: separating closely packed fibres in the preparatory stages of spinning.

package: assembly of yarn wound onto a support, eg. cone, cheese.

pirn: package on which yarn is wound for use as weft.

spinneret: metal plate perforated with holes through which the fibre-forming substances in either a plastic, molten state, or in solution, are extruded during the manufacture of man made fibres.

spinning: the process or processes used in the production of spun and filament yarns.

spinning system: particular system of processes and machines for spinning particular types of fibre, eg. cotton system, woollen system, worsted system.

stretch breaking: method of cutting continuous filament tow into staple fibres of predetermined length, where the filaments of the tow are broken by progressive stretching between successive sets of rollers.

tow-to-top conversion: process where continuous filaments in the form of tow are converted directly into sliver for the production of spun yarns.

web: sheet of fibres.

B2

woollen system: spinning system developed specifically for wool fibres, but which is now used in addition for other fibres and fibre blends where the fibres are of similar dimensions.

worsted system: spinning system developed specifically for wool fibres, where the fibres are combed to remove short fibres and make the remaining fibres lie more parallel. Used in addition for other fibres and fibre blends where the fibres are of similar dimensions.

B3 Yarn names

bicomponent fibre yarn: yarn made from bicomponent fibres.

bicomponent filament yarn: yarn made from bicomponent filaments.

bicomponent yarn: yarn having two different staple fibre and/or continuous filament components, eg. two singles spun yarns of different fibres twisted together, two singles filament yarns of different fibres twisted together, a filament yarn of one fibre twisted with a spun yarn of another fibre, core-spun yarns, wrap yarns, wrap-spun yarns, man made filament blend yarns.

biconstituent yarn: man made filament yarn where two or more different filaments are spun in the same operation. Also known as co-spun yarn and filament blend yarn.

bouclé yarn: fancy yarn typically showing an irregular pattern of curls or loops.

bulked staple fibre yarn: yarn produced by blending together during spinning staple fibres with high and low shrinkage potential. Hot or wet treatment after spinning produces a high bulk spun yarn. Bicomponent fibres can also be used to produce a bulked staple fibre yarn.

chenille yarn: fancy yarn produced by weaving a leno fabric and cutting into warp-way strips so that each strip forms the yarn, which has a velvety, caterpillar-like appearance.

chiné yarn: originally a 2-fold yarn, one black, one white, giving a regular two colour effect. Term now used to describe any 2-fold, two colour yarn.

cloud yarn: fancy yarn where two differently coloured yarns alternately cover or 'cloud' each other, with the cover colour forming a spiral.

core-spun yarn: yarn where a continuous filament core is surrounded by staple fibres. This maintains the strength and/or elasticity of the core while giving the appearance and handle of a spun yarn, eg. elastane filament core with spun polyamide surrounding the core, cotton and polyester sewing thread with spun cotton surrounding the filament polyester core.

co-spun yarn: man made filament yarn where two or more different filaments are spun in the same operation. Also known as biconstituent yarn and filament blend yarn.

covered yarn: yarn where one yarn under controlled tension is covered or wrapped with one or more other yarns, eg. some elastomeric yarns.

crêpe yarn: spun or filament yarns that are very highly S or Z twisted used for the production of crêpe fabrics.

elastomeric yarn: yarn containing filaments of either elastodiene or elastane polymer, characterised by very high extensibility with complete or near complete recovery.

filament blend yarn: man made filament yarn where two or more different filaments are spun in the same operation. Also known as biconstituent yarn and co-spun yarn.

flake yarn: fancy yarn characterised by irregular patches of flattened slubs.

gimp yarn: fancy yarn with a neat, wavy configuration.

high bulk staple fibre yarn: *see* **bulked staple fibre yarn**.

knickerbocker yarn: fancy yarn characterised by random flecks or spots of differently coloured fibres.

knit-de-knit yarn: textured yarn produced by knitting yarn into fabric, heat setting it, and then unravelling the yarn.

knop yarn: fancy yarn characterised by rounded clumps of yarn arranged at intervals.

loop yarn: fancy yarn characterised by circular loops of yarn projecting from the yarn surface.

marl effect yarn: yarn produced from two single continuous filament yarns of different solid colours twisted together.

marl yarn: yarn consisting of two or more spun single yarns of different colour twisted together.

metallic yarn: yarn which contains metal, usually aluminium, used for decorative effects in fabrics.

nepp yarn: alternative name for knickerbocker yarn.

slub yarn: fancy yarn characterised by areas of thicker, loosely twisted yarn alternating with thinner, harder twisted areas.

snarl yarn: fancy yarn where very highly twisted yarn is introduced as loops which kink or snarl to give a spiky appearance.

spiral yarn: fancy yarn showing smooth coiled areas of varying dimensions.

split-film yarn: yarn made by stretching a film or sheet of plastic until it fibrillates or splits up into a network of fibres. At the same time twisting under tension occurs to form the yarn, eg. polypropylene parcel twine.

stripe yarn: fancy yarn characterised by elongated clumps of yarn arranged at intervals.

tuffle yarn: fancy yarn where several yarns are twisted together to form lumps in continuous succession throughout the yarn.

union yarn: yarn made by twisting together yarns of different fibres, eg. a silk yarn twisted with a cotton yarn.

wrap yarn: yarn where a fibrous yarn is wrapped with one or more other yarns which bind in the projecting fibre ends.

wrap-spun yarn: yarn where a yarn is wrapped round a twistless drafted strand of staple fibres.

Fabrics

C1 General terms relating to fabrics

bolt: customarily accepted length of fabric, which varies according to the type of cloth. Alternative name for piece.

classic fabric: named fabric of a particular type or character, suggesting timelessness and quality, eg. chiffon, brocade, velvet.

cloth: general term which can be used for most textile fabrics.

colourway: one of several combinations of colours used for a particular fabric.

comfort fit: describes a fabric or garment containing a small proportion of elastomeric fibre, usually elastane, which ensures that the garment keeps its shape.

counting glass: small magnifying glass mounted on a stand, the base of which is accurately marked with units of measurement (inches or centimetres) around a central aperture. This enables the accurate counting of the ends and picks per unit length in a woven fabric and of the wales and courses in a knitted fabric. *See* **piece glass**, **linen prover**.

cut: length of fabric in the grey state, usually in the range of 45-90 metres, depending on the type and weight of fabric.

cut pile: pile fabric where the loops of yarn are cut to allow the fibre ends to spread out to form a surface of projecting fibre ends, eg. velvet, corduroy.

drape: how a fabric hangs or falls and how it behaves when folded, pleated or gathered. Drape is affected by the properties of the fibre(s) in the fabric, yarn type, fabric structure, finish and weight.

fabric: cloth made from yarns and/or fibres.

fabric fault: imperfection in cloth, which can arise from any stage in processing between fibre and finished product.

fent: short length of fabric cut from a longer length such as a piece. It may or may not be of imperfect material.

figure: motif or prominent part of a pattern, as distinct from the ground or background.

float: length of yarn on the surface or the back of a woven or knitted cloth that is between intersections.

geotextiles: any permeable textile materials used as an integral part of civil engineering structures of earth, rock and other constructional materials, for the purposes of filtration, drainage, separation, reinforcement or stabilisation.

ground: background part of the design in a fabric. Also the structure that forms the main body of the cloth.

ground yarns: those yarns in a fabric that form the base structure of the fabric, eg. in a woven pile fabric the ground warp and weft yarns form the foundation of the fabric and hold the pile yarns firmly in place.

handle: how a textile feels when touched with the hand, eg. warm, rough, soft, smooth, cool.

industrial textiles: textile materials and products intended for end uses other than clothing, household, furnishing and floorcovering. *See* **technical textiles**.

interlining: fabric used between the inner and outer layers of a garment to improve shape retention, strength, warmth or bulk. Interlinings may be woven, knitted or nonwoven, and can be produced with fusible adhesive on one surface.

linen prover: *see* **counting glass**.

lining: fabric used in making garments and other articles, where its properties do not modify the main fabric but do enhance the performance properties of the article as a whole.

loop pile: uncut pile yarn in a pile fabric, eg. terry-towelling.

motif: figure or prominent part of a pattern, as distinct from the ground or background.

narrow fabric: any fabric that does not exceed 45 cms in width (in UK). In the USA and Europe the accepted upper width is 30 cms. Ribbons, tapes, braids and narrow laces are included in this category.

off-grain: general term used to describe faulty fabric in which the warp and weft, although straight, are not at right angles to each other.

one-way fabric: fabric that appears different when viewed from the top and the bottom, ie. along the grain. A number of factors can make a fabric one-way, eg. pattern, nap, pile. When a one-way fabric is cut for making-up it must be used with all the pieces lying in the same direction.

pattern: generally a repeating design, although pattern may be random, ie. there is no exact repeating unit.

piece: customarily accepted length of fabric, which varies according to the type of cloth. *See* **bolt**.

piece glass: *see* **counting glass**.

pile: a surface effect on a fabric formed by loops or tufts of yarn that stand up from the body of the fabric.

pile fabric: a fabric where, during its construction, some yarns are raised up to form the pile, which may be of cut and/or uncut loops.

pile yarns: those yarns in a fabric which form the pile.

reversible: describes fabric that has appropriate pattern and finish on both sides, so that either surface could be used as the face side.

run-of-the-mill fabric: fabric bought from the mill with an agreed allowance for faults.

scrim: general term, irrespective of structure, for a lightweight basecloth.

C1

standard fabric: known, commonly found fabric where the specifications, eg. fibre(s), yarn type and count, fabric construction, finish, weight are generally accepted, eg. poplin, voile, organza, foulard. Often standard fabrics are interpreted by manufacturers using different specifications but retaining the visual characteristics of the original.

stretch fabric: fabric showing greater than usual extensibility and recovery.

technical textiles: textile materials and products manufactured primarily for their technical performance and functional properties rather than their aesthetic or decorative characteristics.

ticking: general term applied to fabrics used for mattress covers, pillows, etc.

traditional name: generally accepted name for a classic or standard fabric type, eg. denim, chambray, cavalry twill.

uncut pile: surface on a fabric consisting of loops of yarn.

union fabric: a fabric made with a warp of one fibre and a weft of a different fibre, eg. a cotton warp with a wool weft, or a linen warp with a cotton weft.

wadding: lofty sheet of fibres used for padding, stuffing or packing.

C2 Terms relating to weaving

beating-up: the movement of the weft yarn or pick into the main body of the woven cloth by the movement of the reed forward to the front of the loom. The third of the three basic operations that occur in weaving.

bias: the angle of 45 degrees to both warp and weft yarns.

cloth roller: the roller on a loom onto which the woven fabric is wound.

dent: part of the reed which comprises one reed wire and the space between two adjacent wires.

dobby: mechanism for controlling the movement of the heald shafts of a loom. Dobby looms can produce more complex patterning than tappet looms, but cannot produce the extremely complex patterning possible on jacquard looms.

ends: the warp yarns that run the whole length of the woven fabric, and lie parallel to the selvedges.

fell: the edge of the cloth in a loom formed by the last beaten-up weft yarn.

grain: the direction in a fabric parallel to the warp yarns and the selvedges.

heald: looped cord, shaped wire or flat metal strip with an eye in the centre, through which a warp yarn or end is threaded so that its movement may be controlled during weaving.

heald frame: rectangular frame which holds a number of healds. Alternative name for shaft.

interlacing: the relative positions of the warp and weft yarns in a woven cloth. The order of interlacing gives the weave or pattern.

jacquard:
(1) a type of loom where the patterning mechanism allows individual control on any interlacing of up to several hundred warp threads.
(2) a fabric woven on a jacquard loom.

left-hand twill: twill where the diagonal runs upwards from bottom-right to top-left on the face of the cloth.

let-off: the gradual unwinding of warp yarn from the warp beam during weaving.

loom: a weaving machine.

mail: central portion of the heald containing the eye or hole through which the warp yarn is threaded.

picking: the insertion of the weft yarn or pick through the shed. The second of the three basic operations that occur in weaving.

picks: the weft yarns that run across the fabric from selvedge to selvedge.

plain weave: most common and simplest woven structure where each warp yarn or end runs over one pick and under the next pick, and each weft yarn or pick runs over one end and under the next.

race: the part of the sley, in front of the reed and below the warp, along which the shuttle containing the weft passes during picking.

reed: comb-like part of the loom which separates and spaces the warp yarns or ends, and beats up the newly-inserted pick or weft yarn into the main body of the cloth.

right-hand twill: twill where the diagonal runs upwards from bottom-left to top-right on the face of the cloth.

selvedge: the neat, firm, longitudinal edge of a woven fabric, parallel to the warp yarns and grain. The purpose of the selvedges is to prevent fraying of the outside ends from the body of the fabric, and to give the edges of the fabric sufficient strength for subsequent processing.

shaft: rectangular frame which holds a number of healds. Alternative name for heald frame.

shed: the space formed by the vertical separation of some warp yarns or ends from other warp yarns or ends.

shedding: the vertical separation of some ends or warp yarns from other ends or warp yarns to form the shed, with the reed towards the back of the loom. The first of the three basic operations that occur in weaving.

shuttle: yarn-package carrier that passes through the shed to insert weft during weaving.

shuttle box: compartment at each end of the sley for retaining the shuttle in the correct position before and after picking.

size: substances put onto warp yarns to strengthen and lubricate them for the strains of weaving.

sizing: process of applying size to warp yarns.

sley: moving part of the loom which carries the reed and the race, situated between the heald shafts and the fell of the cloth.

starch: carbohydrate component extracted from certain plants and used for sizing yarns in weaving, and in finishing to improve the appearance and handle of some fabrics.

take-up: the gradual winding of the cloth onto the cloth roller during weaving.

tappet: cam mechanism for controlling the movement of the heald shafts of a loom. Used for weaving simple constructions.

temple: device on a loom at the fell which holds the fabric as near as possible to the width of the warp in the reed.

twill: a woven fabric with a twill weave where diagonal lines show on the surface of the fabric.

twill weave: weave pattern where the interlacing of the yarns shows a diagonal pattern on the cloth.

C2

warp: the longitudinal yarns in a woven fabric parallel to the selvedges.

warp beam: roller placed at the back of the loom containing the warp yarns.

warp float: a length of warp yarn on the back or surface of the cloth that is between intersections.

warp yarn: the yarn that is used in the warp of a woven fabric.

weave: the order in which the warp and weft yarns interlace in one repeat of the pattern.

weaving: method of constructing cloth by interlacing warp and weft yarns.

weft: the yarns in a woven fabric that run widthways, ie. from selvedge to selvedge.

weft float: a length of weft yarn on the back or surface of the cloth that is between intersections.

weft yarn: the yarn that is used in the weft of a woven fabric.

C3 Terms relating to knitting

alternate gating: the alternate alignment of one set of needles with another set of needles in a machine where the two sets of needles are arranged to knit rib fabric. Also known as rib gating.

bearded needle: type of machine knitting needle, where the open hook can be closed by an action known as pressing.

circular knitting machine: weft knitting machine where the needles are set in a circular bed so that the fabric produced is tubular.

compound needle: type of machine knitting needle, with two operating parts which enable the hook of the needle to be open or closed.

courses: the rows of loops in a warp or weft knitted fabric that run across the width of the fabric.

double-ended needle: needle for machine knitting with a latch (or a beard) at each end. Used on purl knitting machines.

effect side: the side of the fabric which will be used as the face of the cloth. This may or may not be the same as the technical face of the fabric. Sometimes the technical back is the surface that shows in the final product.

fashioned / fully fashioned: describes weft knitted fabrics or garments that are partly or wholly shaped by widening or narrowing the width of the fabric being knitted. This is done by loop transference and increasing or decreasing the number of needles actually knitting.

flat knitting machine: weft knitting machine with straight needle beds, usually with latch needles. Flat fabrics, as opposed to circular, are produced.

float loop: length of yarn not received by a needle and connecting two loops of the same course that are not in adjacent wales. Also known as missed loop.

float stitch: stitch where the yarn is not received by a needle and floats across connecting two loops on the same course that are not in adjacent wales. Also known as missed stitch.

gating: the relative alignment of two sets of knitting elements, eg. needles, on a knitting machine.

gauge: term giving an indication of the number of needles per unit length in a knitting machine.

guide bar: bar running the full width of a warp knitting machine onto which are mounted the yarn guides. The patterning device on the machine controls the movement of the guide bar, and thus the movement of the yarns from needle to needle.

hand knitting: process of knitting by using both hands and two or more hand knitting needles, usually made from steel, wood or plastic.

held loop: loop which, having been pulled through the loop of the previous course, is retained by the needle during the knitting of one or more additional courses.

hosiery: knitted articles for covering the feet and legs, eg. stockings, tights and socks.

inlaid yarn: a yarn in a knitted fabric which has not been knitted, but is held in place in the fabric by the knitted loops. Fabrics produced with laid-in or inlay yarns may be weft knitted or warp knitted.

inlay: technique of incorporating an inlaid yarn into a knitted structure.

intarsia: weft knit technique where different colours are used within plain, rib or purl structures on the same course. Each area of colour is knitted from a separate yarn which is contained in that area and does not float on the back of the fabric.

interlock: weft knit double jersey structure consisting of two interconnected rib fabrics. The simplest and most commonly found interlock structure is 1 and 1 interlock. This shows wales of plain knitting on both sides of the fabric.

interlock gating: the opposed alignment of one set of needles with another set of needles in a machine where the two sets of needles are arranged to knit interlock fabric. Also known as opposite gating.

knit-de-knit: process of knitting a fabric, treating it to produce a particular effect, and unravelling the fabric. *See* **knit-de-knit yarn**, **space dyeing**.

knitting: the process of forming a fabric by the intermeshing of loops of yarn.

knitwear: general term applied to all outerwear knitted garments except stockings, tights and socks.

knock-over: the action of casting off the old loop over the head of the needle.

laid-in yarn: a yarn in a knitted fabric which has not been knitted, but is held in place in the fabric by the knitted loops. Fabrics produced with laid-in or inlay yarns may be warp knitted or weft knitted.

latch needle: type of machine knitting needle, where a small hook at the top of the needle can be closed by a pivoting latch.

laying-in: technique of incorporating a laid-in or inlay yarn into a knitted structure.

loop: basic unit of the knitted structure.

missed loop: length of yarn not received by a needle and connecting two loops of the same course that are not in adjacent wales. Also known as float loop.

missed stitch: stitch where the yarn is not received by a needle, and floats across connecting two loops on the same course that are not in adjacent wales. Also known as float stitch.

needle: instrument used for intermeshing loops. In machine knitting there is usually one needle for each wale in the fabric.

needle bar: assembly of needles in a warp knitting machine.

needle bed: assembly of needles in a weft knitting machine.

opposite gating: the opposed alignment of one set of needles with another set of needles in a machine where the two sets of needles are arranged to knit interlock fabric. Also known as interlock gating.

overlap: the yarn that goes over the hook of the needle. The overlaps show on the face of a knitted fabric made on one set of needles.

plain: weft knitted fabric made on one set of needles where all the loops mesh in the same direction. Also known as single jersey. A different appearance shows on the face and back of the fabric.

plated fabric: fabric knitted from two yarns with different properties, both of which are used in the same loop whilst positioned one behind the other. Each loop exhibits the characteristics of one yarn on the face side of the fabric and the characteristics of the other yarn on the reverse side.

purl: weft knitted fabric where the loops on every wale at each needle on some courses are intermeshed to the front of the fabric, and on the remaining courses the loops on every wale are intermeshed to the back of the fabric. A similar appearance shows on the face and back of the fabric.

raschel machine: warp knitting machine with great versatility because both filament and spun yarns may be used, and up to fifty guide bars give enormous scope for patterning.

rib: weft knitted fabric, made on machines with two sets of needles, where all the loops on some wales are intermeshed to the front of the fabric and all the loops on the remaining wales are intermeshed to the back of the fabric.

rib gating: the alternate alignment of one set of needles with another set of needles in a machine where the two sets of needles are arranged to knit rib fabric. Also known as alternate gating.

shogging: sideways or lateral movement of the guide bar parallel to the needle bar of a warp knitting machine. Produces overlaps on the technical front of the fabric and underlaps on the technical back.

spirality: distortion in a weft knitted fabric where the wales and/or the courses do not follow a true vertical and true horizontal direction respectively. Wale spirality is caused by twist-lively yarn on either a circular knitting machine or a flat knitting machine. Course spirality is caused by multiple feeds on a circular knitting machine.

stitch pattern: knitted structure where the intermeshing of the knitted loops is defined, eg. 6x3 rib, 2-bar tricot.

stitches: intermeshed loops in a knitted fabric.

straight-bar machine: weft knitting machine with bearded needles fixed in a moveable straight bar or bars, used to produce fashioned or fully-fashioned goods.

technical back: the side of a knitted fabric that shows the underlaps.

technical face: the side of a knitted fabric that shows the overlaps.

tricot machine: warp knitting machine used to make fine lightweight fabrics from filament yarns, using no more than four warp beams and guide bars.

tuck loop: a length of yarn received by a needle and not pulled through the loop of the previous course.

tuck stitch: stitch consisting of a held loop and a tuck loop, both of which are intermeshed in the same course.

underlap: the yarn that joins the loops together. The underlaps show on the back of a knitted fabric made on one set of needles.

C3

wales: the columns of loops in a warp or weft knitted fabric that run along the length of the fabric.

warp: the sheet(s) of yarns from which warp knitted fabrics are constructed.

warp knitted: describes a fabric made on a warp knitting machine.

warp knitting: method of constructing a knitted fabric where the loops made from each warp yarn are formed substantially along the length of the fabric. Each warp yarn is fed more or less in line with the direction in which the fabric is produced.

weft knitted: describes a flat or circular fabric made on a weft knitting machine.

weft knitting: method of constructing a knitted fabric where the loops made from each weft yarn are formed substantially across the width of the fabric. Each weft yarn is fed more or less at right angles to the direction in which the fabric is produced, and the fabric may be flat or tubular depending on the machine used.

welt: secure edge of a knitted fabric or garment, made during or after the knitting process.

yarn guide: element on a machine which controls and guides the yarn, eg. in warp knitting each warp yarn passes through a yarn guide.

Fabrics

C4 Woven and knitted fabrics

accordion fabric: weft knitted fabric, with a figured design in two or more colours, that is produced on one set of needles by knitting and missing, and where long floats on the back of the fabric are avoided by introducing tuck stitches.

Argyll: pattern originating in Scotland, showing blocks of solid colour, often geometric. Produced by intarsia knitting, much used for sweaters and socks.

atlas: warp knitted fabric characterised by having one or more sets of yarns traversing in a diagonal manner, one wale per course for a number of courses, returning in the same manner to the original wale. *See* also **single atlas** and **double atlas**.

barathea: fabric with pebbled appearance, usually a twilled hopsack or broken-rib weave, and made of silk, worsted wool or man made fibres. Used for a variety of clothing products, including men's suitings.

batiste: fine, soft, plain weave fabric traditionally made from linen, now often made with other fibres, especially cotton.

Bedford cord: woven structure showing pronounced rounded cords running in the warp direction due to the particular weave.

birdseye:
(1) colour-and-weave effect where the pattern shows small, uniform spots.
(2) the reverse side of a flat-jacquard weft knitted fabric where the yarns are arranged to show minimum amounts of each colour in an all-over pattern.

blister fabric: weft knitted, rib-based fabric showing a three-dimensional puckered figure in relief on a flat ground. Also known as relief fabric and cloqué fabric.

Fabrics: Woven and knitted fabrics

bourrelet: non-jacquard double jersey weft knit structure made on an interlock basis showing horizontal ridges on the effect side.

brocade: figured woven jacquard fabric, usually multicoloured, much used for furnishings.

buckram: plain weave fabric, generally of linen or cotton, which is stiffened during finishing with fillers and starches. Uses include interlinings and bookbinding fabrics.

buckskin: woven fabric made from fine Merino wool, with a dress-face finish. The appearance and handle resemble doeskin but the fabric is heavier.

calico: general term for plain cotton fabrics heavier than muslin. These are usually left unbleached, are made in a variety of weights, and are often used for making toiles.

cambric: lightweight, closely woven, plain weave fabric, usually made from cotton or linen.

canvas: strong, firm, relatively heavy and rigid, generally plain woven cloth traditionally made from cotton, linen, hemp or jute.

cardigan-full: variation of 1 and 1 rib, where every stitch in the wales on both sides of the fabric consists of a held loop and a tuck loop. Also known as polka rib.

cardigan-half: variation of 1 and 1 rib, where every stitch in the wales on one side of the fabric consists of a knitted loop, and every stitch in the wales on the opposite side of the fabric consists of a tuck loop and a held loop. Also known as royal rib.

cavalry twill: firm woven fabric with a steep twill showing double twill lines, traditionally used for riding breeches and jodphurs.

challis: lightweight, plain weave, worsted-spun fabric, generally of wool, with a soft handle and good drape. It is often printed.

chambray: lightweight, plain weave cotton cloth with a dyed warp and a white weft.

cheese cloth: open, lightweight, plain weave fabric with a slightly crêpey appearance, usually made from carded cotton yarns with higher than average twist.

Cheviot tweed: tweed made from Cheviot wool, or wools of similar quality.

chiffon: originally a very lightweight, sheer, plain weave fabric made from silk. Now can also be used to describe a similar fabric using other fibres.

chintz: closely woven, lustrous, plain weave cotton fabric, printed or plain, that has been friction calendered or glazed. Much used for curtainings and upholstery.

ciré: smooth woven or knitted fabric that is impregnated with a synthetic wax and passed through a friction calender. Gives a waxy or wet-look effect. Can also be achieved with heat alone on thermoplastic fibre fabrics.

clip-spot fabric: extra-warp or extra-weft fabric where the yarn floating between the small spots of pattern is clipped or sheared off after weaving by a scissor-like device.

cloqué:
(1) particular type of woven double cloth where the two sets of warp and weft yarns have very different shrinkage potentials, allowing the production in finishing of figured blister effects.
(2) weft knitted, rib-based double jersey fabric, showing a three-dimensional puckered figure in relief on a flat ground. Also known as blister fabric and relief fabric.

colour-and-weave effect: pattern produced by combining a particular weave structure, often a simple weave such as plain weave or 2/2 twill, with a specific arrangement of differently coloured yarns. Examples include birdseye, Prince of Wales check and dogstooth check.

colour-woven: fabric where the design of the fabric is based primarily on the effects of using differently coloured yarns in the warp and/or the weft. Examples include gingham and tartan.

C4

corduroy: woven, cut weft-pile fabric where the cut pile runs in vertical cords along the length of the fabric. A number of different types are found, ranging from pincord (very fine cords) to elephant cord (very broad cords).

crêpe: fabric characterised by a crinkled or puckered surface, which can be be produced by a number of methods.
(1) woven fabric where short, irregular floats in warp and weft are arranged to give an all-over, random pattern within the weave repeat.
(2) woven or knitted fabric where the crêpe characteristics are achieved mainly by the use of highly twisted yarns, which in finishing develop the crinkled, puckered appearance of a crêpe.
(3) fabric where the crêpe effect is produced in finishing by treatment with embossing rollers, engraved with a crêpe pattern, which impart a crêpe effect onto the fabric through heat and pressure.

crêpe de chine: lightweight, plain weave crêpe fabric, made with highly twisted continuous filament yarns in the weft, alternating one S and one Z twist, and with normally twisted continuous filament yarns in the warp. The crêpe effect is relatively unpronounced.

crepon: crêpe fabric showing a pronounced fluted or crinkled effect in the warp direction.

cretonne: printed fabric, usually a cotton furnishing, which is heavier than a chintz.

crushed velvet: pile fabric where the pile is laid in different directions in finishing, giving the fabric varied lustre.

damask: figured fabric, originally a single colour, where the figure and the ground are in contrasting weaves, generally warp-satin and weft-sateen. Traditionally used for expensive tablelinen, now also used for fashion, and sometimes made using more than one colour.

delaine: lightweight, printed, all wool plain weave fabric.

denim: hardwearing cotton twill weave fabric with dyed yarn more closely set in the warp, and unbleached, undyed yarn of a coarser count in the weft.

doeskin: woven fabric with excellent handle, lustre and drape, usually made from fine Merino wool, with a dress-face finish, where the fabric is milled, raised and closely cropped.

dogstooth check: colour-and-weave effect produced by combining a 2/2 twill with a 4 and 4 order of colouring in warp and weft. Very small versions of this effect are known as houndstooth check.

Donegal tweed: woollen-spun woven fabric characterised by randomly distributed clumps of brightly coloured fibres in the yarns. A true Donegal tweed is made in County Donegal in Ireland.

double atlas: warp knitted fabric with two sets of yarns making identical single atlas movements but in opposite directions.

double cloth: compound woven fabric where two sets of warp yarns and weft yarns allow the face and back fabrics to show completely different patterns. Some yarns from one fabric interlace with the other fabric so that the fabrics are held together. Alternatively a third, finer, hidden warp interlaces with both fabrics binding them together.

double jersey: general term used to describe weft knitted fabrics made on two sets of needles. Includes both rib-based and interlock-based structures.

double piqué: non-jacquard, double jersey weft knitted fabric made on a rib basis, using a selection of knitted loops and floats.

drill: woven twill fabric with a similar structure to denim, but usually piece-dyed.

eight-lock: non-jacquard, double jersey weft knitted fabric made on an interlock basis and showing a similar appearance on the face and back of the fabric.

extra-warp fabric: woven fabric where an additional set of warp yarns is used to produce patterning.

extra-weft fabric: woven fabric where an additional set of weft yarns is used to produce patterning.

façonné: figured jacquard woven fabric with a pattern of small, scattered motifs. Generally a single colour.

flannel: light to medium weight wool fabric, often grey, of plain or twill weave with a soft handle. It may be slightly milled and raised.

flat-jacquard: patterned flat rib-based weft knitted fabric showing a figure in differing colour and/or texture on the face of the fabric.

foulard: lightweight 2/2 twill fabric, originally of silk, and often printed. Much used for scarves due to its firm, non-slip characteristics.

full cardigan: *see* **cardigan-full**.

gaberdine: steep twill fabric, originally made from worsted wool, where the ends are set much more closely than the picks. Much used for raincoats due to its firm structure and water-repellent properties.

gauze: lightweight, open-textured fabric made in plain weave or a simple leno weave.

georgette: fine, lightweight, plain weave, crêpe fabric, usually having two highly twisted S and two highly twisted Z yarns alternately in both warp and weft.

gingham: lightweight, plain weave, traditionally cotton fabric where dyed and white yarns are arranged to show a pattern of small checks.

grosgrain: plain weave fabric with a pronounced rib in the weft direction, formed by using a relatively fine, continuous filament, closely-set warp and a much coarser weft, producing a characteristic ribbed effect.

half cardigan: *see* **cardigan-half**.

half-Milano rib: weft knitted rib-based double jersey structure.

Harris tweed: woollen-spun tweed fabric, traditionally woven on narrow hand looms on the island of Harris in Scotland. Characterised by subtle colours and a relatively harsh handle.

herringbone: twill fabric where the direction of the twill is reversed, producing a pattern resembling herring bones.

hessian: coarse, plain weave fabric, traditionally made from jute. Used for sacking, wallcoverings and in upholstery.

honeycomb: woven fabric where the interlacing of warp and weft yarns forms ridges and hollows, producing a cellular appearance.

hopsack: variation on plain weave, where two or more ends and picks weave as one. Sometimes called basket weave.

houndstooth check: small colour-and-weave effect produced by a combination of a 2/2 twill and a 4 and 4 order of colouring. Larger versions are known as dogstooth check.

huckaback: woven fabric where short floats of yarn, warp on one side of the cloth, and weft on the other, produce a rough surface effect. Traditionally made from cotton or linen, and much used for roller towels and glass-cloths.

interchanging double cloth: particular kind of woven double cloth where the two fabrics completely interchange at intervals, ie. the top cloth becomes the bottom cloth, and the bottom cloth becomes the top cloth.

interlock: double faced, weft knitted structure consisting of two interconnected rib fabrics. The simplest and most commonly found interlock structure is 1 and 1 interlock. Wales of plain knitting show on both sides of the fabric.

interlock jersey: weft knitted fabric made with an interlock structure.

jacquard fabric:
(1) a fabric woven on a jacquard loom, where the patterning mechanism allows individual control on any interlacing of up to several hundred warp threads.
(2) a rib-based, double jersey weft knit structure which shows a figure or design in a different colour or texture. Jacquard fabrics are sub-divided into flat-jacquard and blister fabrics.

C4

jersey: general term used for any knitted fabric.

knitted fabric: fabric made by the intermeshing of loops of yarn.

lamé: a general name for fabrics where metallic threads are a conspicuous feature.

lawn: fine, plain weave fabric, traditionally of cotton or linen.

leno: woven fabric where some warp yarns are made to diagonally cross other warp yarns between the picks by a special mechanism on the loom. This allows yarns that are widely spaced to be firmly held in place.

locknit: warp knitted tricot fabric, made with two sets of warp yarns. Used extensively for lingerie.

marquisette: square-hole, warp knitted net.

melton: heavyweight fabric, all wool, or with a cotton warp and a woollen weft, usually made in 2/2 twill. The fabric is heavily milled, raised and cropped.

milanese: warp knitted fabric containing twice as many yarns as there are wales in the fabrics. Any particular yarn transverses the full width of the fabric diagonally and, on reaching the selvedge, tranverses the fabric in the opposite direction.

Milano rib: weft knitted rib-based double jersey structure.

mock leno: woven fabric that imitates the open mesh appearance of a leno fabric by the arrangement of warp and weft yarns.

moiré: fabric which shows a moiré or wavy watermark pattern. This is produced in finishing by calendering, usually on a fabric showing a rib or cord effect in the weft direction. The moiré effect can be achieved either by embossing with a roller engraved with a moiré pattern, or by feeding two layers of fabric face to face through the calender. The effect may be permanent or temporary depending on the fibre(s) and chemicals used.

moquette: firm, woven warp-pile fabric where the pile yarns are lifted over wires, which may or may not have knives. Withdrawal of the wires will give a cut or an uncut pile. Used for upholstery, particularly on public transport vehicles.

moss crêpe: fabric with a characteristic spongy handle made with a moss crêpe weave and S and Z twist moss crêpe yarns. Moss crêpe yarns are made by doubling a normal twist yarn with a high twist yarn. Moss crêpe weaves have a relatively large repeat in both warp and weft directions.

mousseline: general term for very fine, semi-opaque fabrics, finer than muslins, made of silk, wool or cotton.

mull: a soft, plain weave cotton fabric with a relatively open texture, and a soft finish.

muslin: lightweight, open, plain or simple leno weave fabric, usually made of cotton.

non-jacquard fabric: describes a large group of double jersey weft knitted structures, usually produced in plain colours. May be rib-based or interlock-based, depending on the structure. Examples include interlock, single piqué, double piqué, eight-lock, bourrelet and punto di Roma.

nun's veiling: lightweight, clear finished, plain weave fabric, usually made of worsted-spun wool, silk or cotton yarns, and usually dyed black.

ondé: describes a fabric showing a wavy effect produced either by calendering or weaving with a special reed. The term is from the French word for waved.

ondulé: fabric with a wavy effect in the warp direction, produced by weaving with a special reed.

organdie: lightweight, plain weave transparent fabric, with a permanently stiff finish.

organza: a sheer, lightweight, plain weave fabric, with a relatively firm drape and handle, traditionally made from fine continuous filament silk yarns. Now often made using other fibres.

panné velvet: pile fabric where the pile is laid in one direction during finishing to give a very high lustre.

percale: closely woven plain weave fabric, often of Egyptian cotton, lighter in weight than chintz.

piqué:
(1) woven fabric showing pronounced rounded cords running in the weft direction, due to the particular weave.
(2) *see* **single piqué** and **double piqué**.

piquette: weft knitted interlock-based double jersey structure.

plaid: *see* **tartan**. Also name for the shawl or wrap of Highland costume, usually a tartan.

plissé: describes fabrics with a puckered or crinkled effect. From the French word for pleated.

plush: woven pile fabric with a longer and less dense pile than velvet. Warp and weft knitted plush fabrics are also produced, with cut or uncut pile, depending on the fabric.

polka rib: variation of 1 and 1 rib, where every stitch consists of a held loop and a tuck loop. Also known as full cardigan.

ponte-Roma: weft knitted, non-jacquard, interlock-based double jersey structure. Alternative name for punto di Roma.

poplin: medium-weight, plain weave fabric, traditionally made from cotton, with a closer set warp than weft. Shows slight weftways ribs, and is much used for shirtings.

Prince of Wales check: colour-and-weave effect much used in men's suitings. Many variations, particularly in scale, are commonly found. Colouring is often grey/white/black, with fine red lines as overchecks.

punto di Roma: weft knitted, non-jacquard, interlock-based double jersey structure. Alternative name for ponte-Roma.

purl: weft knitted structure where both face and reverse loops are used on some or all of the wales, eg. 1 and 1 purl consists of alternate courses of face loops and reverse loops, showing the same pattern on both sides of the fabric.

queenscord: warp knitted two-bar tricot structure.

raschel fabric: warp knitted fabric made on a raschel warp knitting machine. Fabrics can range from fine laces and nets to thick outerwear fabrics.

repp: plain weave fabric with a pronounced weftways rib effect, obtained by using a relatively fine warp and a heavier count weft.

reverse locknit: warp knitted tricot fabric, made with two sets of warp yarns.

rib: weft knitted structure where all the loops on some wales are intermeshed to the front of the fabric and all the loops on the remaining wales are intermeshed to the back of the fabric.

royal rib: variation of 1 and 1 rib, where the wales on one side of the fabric consist wholly of knitted loops, and the wales on the opposite side of the fabric consist of tuck loops and held loops. Also known as half cardigan.

sailcloth: originally a tightly woven linen or cotton canvas used for the manufacture of ship and yacht sails. Now more commonly made from polyamide, polyester and aramid fibres.

sateen: woven structure where the maximum amount of weft shows on the face. The smooth effect is enhanced by using filament yarns and/or lustrous fibres.

satin: woven structure where the maximum amount of warp shows on the face. The smooth effect is enhanced by using filament yarns and/or lustrous fibres.

seersucker: fabric characterised by puckered and relatively flat areas, usually in stripes. The effect can be produced in several ways.
(1) a woven seersucker is made by using two warps, one with highly tensioned yarn, and the other with less highly tensioned yarn, in alternate narrow sections across the fabric. During wet finishing the highly tensioned yarns shrink more than the loosely tensioned yarns, causing alternate flat and puckered areas in the fabric.
(2) a cellulosic fibre fabric can be printed in areas with a

C4

solution of sodium hydroxide (caustic soda), which causes the printed areas to contract, leaving the unprinted areas puckered.
(3) yarns with different shrinkage properties can be combined in the warp and/or the weft.

serge: twill fabric, traditionally made from wool, usually piece-dyed. Often used for uniforms.

shantung: plain weave dress fabric showing random yarn irregularities, due originally to the unevenness of the tussah silk filaments. Now often made using different fibres.

sharkskin: firm, slightly stiff, two-bar tricot warp knitted fabric.

shingosen: new generation of sophisticated, technically complex Japanese fabrics with superior aesthetics and handle. Generally made from polyester, combining fibres of different shrinkage rates, cross sections and diameters.

single atlas: warp knitted fabric characterised by having one set of yarns traversing in a diagonal manner, one wale per course for a number of courses, returning in the same manner to the original wale.

single jersey: weft knitted fabric produced on one set of needles, where all the loops in the fabric mesh in the same direction. Fabric made in this way may also be called plain.

single piqué: non-jacquard, double jersey weft knitted fabric made on an interlock basis, using a selection of knitted and tuck loops.

taffeta: plain weave, closely woven, smooth, crisp fabric with a slight weftways rib, originally made from continuous filament silk yarns. Now often made using other fibres.

tartan: originally a woollen fabric of 2/2 twill, woven in checks of various colours, and worn by Scottish clans, each clan having its own distinct pattern. Now descriptive of a wider range of fabrics with this type of patterning. Tartans are sometimes called plaids.

terry-towelling: a woven warp-pile fabric where the loops are formed by applying a high tension to the ground warp and a very low tension to the pile warp. Beating-up does not occur on every pick, so that when a pick is beaten-up it causes the other picks to be moved into the main body of the cloth, at the same time forming the pile loops on the face and back of the cloth.

texipiqué: weft knitted interlock-based double jersey structure.

thornproof tweed: closely woven tweed fabric with highly twisted yarns and a firm, hard handle. Resistant to damage from thorns, and therefore used for clothing for rural activities.

tricot fabric: fine warp knitted fabric made on a tricot warp knitting machine using continuous filament yarns.

tussore: fabric woven from tussah silk.

tweed: originally a coarse, medium to heavy in weight, rough-surfaced, woven wool fabric. Now a term applied many fabrics, of varying constructions and fibre content, showing a characteristic rough, textured surface.

velour:
(1) a heavy pile fabric with the pile laid in one direction.
(2) a napped-surface woven fabric or felt where the surface fibres are laid in one direction to give a smooth appearance.
(3) a warp or weft knitted cut pile fabric.

velour (jersey): cut pile weft or warp knitted fabric.

velvet: cut warp-pile fabric, in which the cut fibrous ends of the yarns form the surface of the fabric. Many effects are possible, eg. the pile may be left erect, or it may be laid in one direction during finishing to give a very high lustre.

velveteen: cut weft-pile fabric where the cut fibrous ends of the yarns form the surface of the fabric.

voile: plain weave, semi-sheer, lightweight fabric made with fine, fairly highly twisted yarns. Originally made from cotton, now other fibres are sometimes used.

warp-pile: describes a fabric where the pile is formed by pile yarns in the warp, eg. velvet, terry-towelling.

weft-pile: describes a fabric where the pile is formed by pile yarns in the weft, eg. corduroy, velveteen.

whipcord: steep twill fabric, commonly made from cotton or worsted-spun wool, where the closely set warp yarns form a cord-like effect.

woven carpeting: pile fabric incorporating a firm substrate or base, making it suitable for use as a floor covering.

woven fabric: fabric made by interlacing two sets of yarns, the warp and the weft.

Fabrics

C5 Terms relating to methods of fabric construction other than weaving and knitting, and fabrics made by these methods

adhesive bonded nonwoven: textile material composed of a web or batt of fibres, bonded together by the application of adhesive. The method of application of the adhesive and the density of the fibre web determine the character of the end product. Also known as bonded fibre fabric.

barbed needle: needle with downwardly pointing indentations designed to entangle fibres within a batt or web when the needle is moved up and down.

batt: single or multiple sheets of fibre, used in the production of nonwovens and felts.

bonded fabric: material composed of two or more layers, at least one of which is a textile fabric. These are bonded closely together with an added adhesive, or by the adhesive properties of one or more of the component layers. Bonded fabrics are also known as laminated fabrics and as combined fabrics.

bonded fibre fabric: textile material composed of a web or batt of fibres, bonded together by the application of adhesive. The method of application of the adhesive and the density of the fibre web determine the character of the end product. Also known as adhesive bonded nonwoven.

braid: narrow fabric made by interlacing three or more yarns diagonally to form a plait. The structure may be flat or tubular, eg. shoelaces. In addition, some types of narrow woven and knitted textiles are described as braids.

candlewick: tufted fabric, generally made from cotton, often used for bedspreads.

C5

coated fabric: material composed of two or more layers, at least one of which is a textile fabric and at least one of which is a substantially continuous polymeric layer. These are bonded closely together with an added adhesive or by the adhesive properties of one or more of the component layers.

combined fabric: material composed of two or more layers, at least one of which is a textile fabric. These are bonded closely together with an added adhesive, or by the adhesive properties of one or more of the component layers. Combined fabrics are also known as laminated fabrics and as bonded fabrics.

felt:
(1) fabric made directly from fibres containing at least 50% of animal hair, usually wool. Manufacture relies on the property of wool and other animal hair fibres to become entangled when exposed to heat, moisture and intermittent mechanical pressure.
(2) fabric woven or knitted from staple fibre yarns containing some wool or animal hair, where in finishing the woven or knitted construction is completely obscured by the smooth felted surface of the fabric.
(3) needlefelt: a nonwoven fabric where fibres are entangled by the mechanical action of barbed needles.

hydroentangled fabric: mechanically bonded nonwoven fabric made by entangling the staple fibres in the batt with high pressure water jets. Also known as spunlaced fabric.

lace: open work fabric usually with a ground of mesh or net on which patterns are worked either as the ground is made or at a later stage. The yarns are looped, twisted or knitted to achieve the openess of the fabric and the pattern. Machine made laces are often named according to the machines on which they have been made, eg. Leavers lace, raschel lace.

laminated fabric: material composed of two or more layers, at least one of which is a textile fabric. These are bonded closely together with an added adhesive, or by the adhesive properties of one or more of the component layers. Laminated fabrics are also known as bonded fabrics and as combined fabrics.

mechanically bonded nonwoven: nonwoven fabric where the fibres in the batt are mechanically entangled to form the fabric. Examples include spunlaced fabrics and needlepunched fabrics.

melded fabric: thermally bonded nonwoven fabric made wholly or partly of bicomponent fibres, where one component softens when heated and sticks the fibres together.

mesh: open fabric formed either by the way in which yarns are twisted around each other or knitted to form holes. The holes in the mesh may be square, hexagonal, rounded or diamond. *See* **net**.

microporous polymer laminate: continuous membrane with extremely small pores or holes, which are big enough to allow the passage of water vapour, but are too small to allow water droplets to penetrate.

needlebonded fabric: alternative name for needlepunched fabric.

needled fabric: alternative name for needlepunched fabric.

needlefelted fabric: alternative name for needlepunched fabric.

needleloom: machine on which needlepunched fabrics are made.

needlepunched fabric: nonwoven mechanically bonded fabric made by using barbed needles which are continuously punched into the fibre web and withdrawn. This causes the fibres to become entangled. Needlepunched fabrics are also known as needlebonded fabrics, needlefelted fabrics and needled fabrics.

net: open mesh fabric where the openess of the fabric is achieved either by the way in which yarns are twisted round each other or knitted to form holes. The holes in the net may be square, hexagonal, rounded or diamond. *See* **mesh**.

nonwoven: term covering textile structures made directly from fibres rather than yarn. Bonding of the fibres to form a fabric is achieved by a number of methods, including adhesive bonding, mechanical bonding, thermal bonding and solvent bonding.

sew-knit fabric: alternative name for stitch-bonded fabric.

smallware: collective name in the textile trade for braids, ribbons and tapes.

solvent bonded nonwoven: nonwoven fabric where the bonding is achieved by using a solvent which softens the fibre surfaces in the web or batt and thus causes bonding.

spunbonded fabric: nonwoven fabric made from continuous filaments which are extruded or spun and formed into a random-laid web in one process. The web is then consolidated into a fabric by adhesive bonding, mechanical bonding, thermal bonding or solvent bonding. Also known as spunlaid fabric.

spunlaced fabric: mechanically bonded nonwoven fabric made by entangling the staple fibres in the batt with high pressure water jets. Also known as hydroentangled fabric.

spunlaid fabric: nonwoven fabric made from continuous filaments which are extruded or spun and formed into a random-laid web in one process. The web is then consolidated into a fabric by adhesive bonding, mechanical bonding, thermal bonding or solvent bonding. Also known as spunbonded fabric.

stitch-bonded fabric: multi-component fabric where one component is a series of interlooped warp knit stitches running the length of the fabric. The other components can be fibres, or yarns, or a combination of both, or pre-formed fabric.

thermally bonded nonwoven: nonwoven fabric where the thermoplastic nature of some or all of the fibres in the web or batt is utilised. The application of heat causes the fibre surfaces to soften and stick together permanently. Sometimes a heat sensitive powder is dispersed within the fibre web to cause bonding.

tufted fabric: fabric where tufts of yarn are inserted with special needles into an already constructed ground fabric. The base fabric can be woven, knitted or nonwoven. The pile loops formed by the tufting machine can be cut or left uncut.

web: single or multiple sheets of fibres. Also known as batt.

Dyeing

D Terms relating to dyeing

acid dye: class of dye used on protein fibres, such as wool and silk, and nylon.

aftertreatment: treatment given to some dyed textiles to improve the colour fastness or some other quality such as brightness.

alum: potassium aluminium sulphate, commonly used as a mordant for natural dyes.

assistant: substance used in the dyeing (or printing) process to aid the colouration.

auxiliary: substance which improves the effectiveness of a dyeing, printing or finishing process.

azoic dye: class of dye used on cellulosic fibres.

basic dye: class of dye used on some acrylics.

batch: lot of textile material (fibre, yarn or fabric) processed at the same time. Important because material from different dye lots or batches can show variation in colour.

batch dyeing: dyeing by processing in lots or batches, where all the material in one batch is subjected to one stage of the process at a time.

bath: vessel in which dyeing takes place.

batik: resist method of patterning cloth where wax is used as the resist. Molten wax is applied to the cloth, traditionally by a hand process, in a pattern and the wax is allowed to harden. The waxed cloth is dyed and the wax removed afterwards. The process can be repeated to build up complex patterns. Sometimes the hardened wax is cracked to produce a characteristic veining.

D

batik dyeing: resist dyeing using wax as the resist. The wax resist is sometimes applied by printing. Other resists are traditionally used in different parts of the world.

beam dyeing machine: machine for dyeing where the textile material is wound on a perforated roller or beam through which the dye-liquor is circulated.

beck: open topped vessel containing liquid used for treating textile materials, eg. dyes in solution.

bleeding: loss of colorant from a coloured textile material in contact with a liquor, leading to an obvious colouration of the liquor, and/or adjacent areas of the same or other materials.

blue standards: standard samples of wool fabric dyed with specified blue dyes with known rates of fading. Used for light fastness assessment. Rating is on a scale of 1 to 8, where 1 shows very poor fastness and 8 shows extremely good fastness.

changeant: effect where the colour of the fabric appears to change when viewed from a different angle. Produced either by cross dyeing where the warp and weft are different fibres and are dyed with different dyes, or by using dyed yarns where the warp is one colour and the weft is another colour. Also known as a shot effect, and as a two-tone effect.

chrome dye: class of dyes used on wool.

coal-tar dye: old name for synthetic dyes because it was coal-tar from coal which provided the colourless materials from which the highly coloured organic substances, called dyes, were originally manufactured.

cochineal: natural red dye from a South American beetle.

colorant: a colouring matter, which may be a dye or a pigment.

colour-spun (fibre): man made fibre coloured by putting the colorant into the spinning solution before extrusion of the filaments through the spinneret.

colour-spun yarn: yarn made from fibres, staple or filament, that have already been dyed.

colour-woven: woven fabric where differently coloured yarns are used in the warp and/or the weft, eg. tartan, gingham.

continuous dyeing: dyeing by processing the textile material in sequence through a series of stages to give a continuous output of processed material.

converter: textile company or individual that purchases grey cloth and finishes it, including dyeing and/or printing, and then sells the finished fabric.

crocking: abrasive action on a textile to which dyes and pigments have a measurable fastness. Alternative name for rubbing.

cross dyeing: the dyeing of a component in a mixture of fibres of which at least one is coloured separately.

deep-dye: describes fibres that have been modified to have a greater uptake of dye compared with the unmodified fibres. Also used to describe a process for dyeing or printing carpets with complete penetration of the pile.

deep-dyeing fibres: *see* **deep-dye**.

differential dyeing fibres: fibres modified to dye with a different class of dye from that used for the unmodified fibre. Allows cross dyeing within the same fibre group. Also known as dye-variant fibres.

direct dye: class of dye used on cellulosic fibres.

disperse dye: class of dye used on some man made synthetic and modified cellulosic fibres, eg. polyester, acetate and triacetate.

dope: solution of fibre-forming polymer before extrusion through the spinneret.

dope-dyed: *see* **mass colouration**.

dye: highly coloured organic substance which can be absorbed and retained by a fibre so that the textile product remains permanently coloured.

D

dyebath: vessel in which dyeing takes place.

dyeing: the application and fixation of dye to a textile, as fibre, yarn, fabric or garment, usually to give a level or even shade.

dyestuff: alternative name for dye.

dye-lot: batch of dyed material that has been processed as one, ie. dyed in the same dyebath with identical treatment from beginning to end of the dyeing process.

dye-variant fibres: fibres modified to dye with a different class of dye from that used for the unmodified fibre. Allows cross dyeing within the same fibre group. Also known as differential dyeing fibres.

exhaustion: the proportion of a dye or any other substance taken up by a substrate at any stage of a process from the amount originally available.

fabric-dyed: describes a textile which has been dyed at the fabric stage of processing. More commonly described as piece-dyed.

fading: colour change on a textile, caused by light, washing or a number of other agencies. The change in colour may be in hue, depth or brightness, or in any combination of these.

fast: describes a colorant that has good resistance to fading.

fastness: measurable quality of a colorant, that indicates how well the colorant resists fading from various agencies, eg. light, washing, rubbing, dry-cleaning.

ferrous sulphate: common mordant used with natural dyes.

fibre dyeing: dyeing of the textile at the fibre stage of processing. Fibres may be dyed in bale form, as loose fibre, tow, slubbing, roving, top or sliver. Also known as stock dyeing.

fugitive: describes a colorant that is not fast.

fugitive tint: colorant that is not fast that is applied to textiles to aid identification during handling. It is removed easily at a later stage. Also known as sighting colour and tinting colour.

garment dyeing: dyeing of textile as made-up garments or parts of garments. Allows colours to be chosen late in the manufacturing cycle as dictated by fashion.

gas fume fading: irreversible change in colour which occurs when some fibres, particularly cellulose acetate, cellulose triacetate and polyamide, dyed with particular disperse dyes, are exposed to oxides of nitrogen produced by use of gas heaters.

grey scales: series of neutral grey colour chips or colour cards, showing increased contrast between pairs. Used to visually assess contrasts between other pairs of patterns, eg. the magnitude of change in colour of a specimen undergoing a fastness test, and the degree of staining of uncoloured adjacent material. Rating is on a scale of 1 to 5, where 1 shows very poor fastness and 5 shows extremely good fastness.

hank-dyed: yarn that is dyed as yarn while wound in hanks, after yarn manufacture and before fabric manufacture.

high-temperature dyeing (HT dyeing): dyeing under superatmospheric presssure whereby the temperature of the dye-liquor is raised above its normal boiling point.

ikat: resist method of patterning yarn for warp and/or weft in a woven fabric. Predetermined sections of yarn are bound tightly before dyeing to prevent penetration of the dye into the tied sections. When woven the cloth shows characteristic blurred edges to the pattern, partly from the movement or redistribution of the warp when put onto the loom, and partly from bleeding and capillary action in the dyeing.

ikat dyeing: *see* **ikat**.

indigo: natural dark blue dye from the indigo plant. Now manufactured synthetically, and much used for the dyeing of denim for jeans owing to its tendency to fade.

injection (dyeing): method of space dyeing where different dyes are injected into cones of yarn through hollow needles.

jet dyeing machine: machine for dyeing fabric in rope form where the movement of the dye-liquor causes the movement of the fabric around the machine.

jig: machine in which fabric in open width is transferred back and forth from one roller to another and passes through a relatively small amount of dye-liquor or other liquid.

jigger: *see* **jig**.

kermes: natural red plant dye.

knit-de-knit: method of space dyeing where yarn is weft knitted into fabric and printed with diagonal stripes of colour. After dye fixation the fabric is unravelled and the yarn wound as usual for processing into cloth.

level shade: even colouration over the surface of the textile.

liquor: general term used in textiles, especially in dyeing, printing and finishing, for liquid (usually water) containing dissolved chemicals used in processing. The term can be made more specific, eg. dye-liquor.

logwood: natural black plant dye.

madder: natural red plant dye.

marking-off: undesirable transfer of colour from one coloured material to another fabric.

mass colouration: method of colouring man made fibres by putting the colorant into the spinning solution before extrusion so that coloured filaments are spun. Fibres coloured by this method may be described as colour-spun, spun-dyed, dope-dyed, solution-dyed, spun-coloured or spun-pigmented.

match: two samples where the colour of one is identical, or very close, to the colour of the other.

mauveine: first synthetic dye discovered in 1856 by William Henry Perkin. Also known as Perkin's mauve.

metameric match: satisfactory match of two colours under one set of lighting conditions, but not satisfactory when the lighting conditions are altered.

metamerism: phenomenon where two colours may match in some lighting conditions but not match in others, eg. daylight and tungsten-filament light. Colours will only match in all lighting conditions if same dyes mixed in the same proportions have been used.

migration: the movement of an added substance, eg. a dye, from one part of a textile material to another.

mordant: chemical compound, usually a metallic salt, which will form a complex link or bridge with a dye and be retained more firmly by a textile than the dye itself. Mordants are commonly used with natural dyes.

mordant dye: dye that is fixed with a mordant. Alternative name for chrome dye.

naphthol dye: class of dye used on cellulosics.

natural dye: dye derived from natural sources: plant, animal or mineral.

nip rollers: pair of rollers between which the textile passes. Often used in wet processes to control the amount of liquor going onto the textile.

off-shade: describes a match that is not commercially acceptable.

ombré: describes any fabric with a dyed, printed or woven design in which the colour is graduated from light to dark. The term is from the French word for shaded, and both shaded designs and shaded fabrics may be called ombré.

on-shade: describes a match that is commercially acceptable.

overdyeing: redyeing of already dyed textile to change the colour.

package-dyed: describes textiles that have been dyed on a package, eg. yarn on perforated cones and cheeses, warp yarn on a perforated warp beam.

paddle dyeing machine: machine used for dyeing garments, where gently moving paddles ensure the circulation of dye-liquor and the even dyeing of the garments.

perforated beam: beam or roller, with holes through which dye-liquor or steam can be passed, onto which the fabric is wound.

Perkin's mauve: first synthetic dye discovered in 1856 by William Henry Perkin. Also known as mauveine.

piece: fabric of commonly accepted length from the loom or knitting machine.

piece dyeing: dyeing at the fabric stage of processing.

piece-dyed: describes fabric which has been dyed at the fabric stage of processing.

pigment: insoluble colour, which can be applied to textiles by mechanically dispersing very fine particles of the pigment in a medium, and fixing to the cloth with a suitable heat-setting resin.

polychromatic dyeing: dyeing process using jets of dye-liquor passing down an inclined plane onto the moving cloth. These jets are mounted on oscillating or sideways-moving carriages. By varying the colours, the degree of oscillation, the concentration of dye and the speed of the cloth, numerous multicolour effects are possible.

potassium aluminium sulphate: common mordant used for natural dyes. Also known as alum.

potassium dichromate: common mordant used for natural dyes.

random dyeing: form of space dyeing where the method ensures that the colouration in the final fabric is random, eg. injection dyeing.

reactive dye: class of dye used on cellulosic and protein fibres.

reserved: describes the property of a dye in a particular dyeing system which allows one or more fibres in a multi-fibre textile to remain uncoloured.

resist: substance applied to a textile to prevent the uptake and fixation of dye in a subsequent dyeing or printing process.

resist dyeing: dyeing of fabric or yarn where a physical or chemical resist has been applied prior to dyeing. Examples include ikat, batik and tie-dyeing.

rubbing: agency to which dyes and pigments have a measurable fastness.

saffron: natural yellow plant dye.

shade: term loosely employed in the dyeing industry to describe a particular colour or depth, eg. pale shade, fashion shade, mode shade.

shot: effect where the colour of the fabric appears to change when viewed from a different angle. Produced either by cross dyeing where the warp and weft are different fibres and are dyed with different dyes, or by using dyed yarns where the warp is one colour and the weft is another colour. Also known as a changeant effect, and as a two-tone effect.

sighting colour: colorant that is not fast that is applied to textiles to aid identification during handling. It is removed easily at a later stage. Also known as fugitive tint and tinting colour.

soaping-off: aftertreatment of dyed or printed textiles with soap or a detergent to remove excess dye and other reagents.

solution-dyed: *see* **mass colouration**.

space dyeing: production of random or regular multi-colour effects on yarn by applying colorants at intervals along the yarn. Alternative methods of space dyeing include injection dyeing and knit-de-knit.

spun-coloured: *see* **mass colouration**.

spun-dyed: *see* **mass colouration**.

spun-pigmented: *see* **mass colouration**.

staining:
(1) undesirable local discolouration caused by accident in processing or use.

(2) in colour fastness testing, the transfer of colorant from the sample being tested to adjacent white material.

(3) in textile printing, the soiling of areas of the cloth during washing-off.

stannous chloride: common mordant used with natural dyes.

stock dyeing: dyeing of a textile at the fibre stage of processing. Fibres may be dyed in bale form, as loose fibre, tow, slubbing, roving, top or sliver. Also known as fibre dyeing.

stripping: removal of dye or finish from a textile.

substantivity: attraction between a dye and a textile fibre, allowing the dye to be absorbed and permanently retained by the fibre.

substrate: a material to which dyes and chemicals may be applied.

sulphur dye: class of dye used on cellulosic fibres.

synthetic dye: dye manufactured from building up complex organic coloured substances from simpler colourless substances obtained as by-products from crude oil.

tendering: local deterioration in a fabric caused by adverse reaction between the dye on the fabric and an agency such as light.

thermochromism: change in colour of certain materials on exposure to heat which is reversible when the temperature is returned to its original value.

tie-dye: resist method of patterning cloth by tying, stitching or knotting the fabric before dyeing. After dyeing the cloth is undone to reveal the pattern. The cloth can be retied and dyed to produce more complex patterns.

tie-dyeing: *see* **tie-dye**.

tinting colour: colorant that is not fast that is applied to textiles to aid identification during handling. It is removed easily at a later stage. Also known as fugitive tint and sighting colour.

tone-in-tone dyeing: dyeing where some fibres have been modified to take up greater amounts of dye than the normal or standard fibres, eg. deep-dye nylon and ultra-deep-dye nylon. When combined with standard fibres and piece-dyed the cloth will show three different shades of the same colour. Also known as tone-on-tone dyeing.

tone-on-tone dyeing: *see* **tone-in-tone dyeing**.

two-tone: *see* **shot** or **changeant**.

Tyrian purple: natural purple animal dye, historically the Imperial purple used for togas in the Roman Empire.

ultra-deep-dye: describes fibres that have been modified to have a much greater uptake of dye compared with the unmodified fibres.

union dyeing: dyeing of a combination of different types of fibres to achieve a single solid colour.

vat dye: class of dye used on cellulosic fibres.

wax: substance used as the mechanical resist in batik dyeing and printing.

winch: machine used for dyeing fabric in rope form, where the fabric is joined end to end, passing over a winch or horizontal rotor, usually above the liquor level of the dyebath. The rotation of the winch draws the fabric out of, and passes it back into, the dye-liquor.

winch dyeing: dyeing of fabric using a winch.

woad: natural blue plant dye.

yarn dyeing: dyeing that takes place after spinning and before fabric manufacture. Yarn may be processed as hanks or skeins, wound onto perforated spindles as cones or cheeses, or wound onto perforated warp beams.

yarn-dyed fabric: describes fabric where the yarns have been dyed before fabric manufacture.

Printing

P Terms relating to printing

aftertreatment: treatment of printed cloth after fixation. The fabric is rinsed to remove surplus unfixed dye and chemicals. Often a soaping treatment is given followed by rinsing and drying.

ageing: fixation of dye on the printed fabric by exposing the cloth to hot, moist air. Also known as steaming.

ager: chamber in which ageing takes place. Also known as steamer.

backing cloth: cloth between the fabric to be printed and the printing base. It prevents print paste from soiling the printing base and acts as a support for the cloth being printed.

baking: dry heat fixation treatment, used in pigment printing, and for some dyes.

batik printing: resist printing of cloth, either with metal hand blocks using wax as a resist, or with duplex engraved rollers using rosin as a resist.

blanket: thick, resilient covering for a firm printing base.

block: wooden block on which the design for printing is in relief. The relief may be wood or hammered-in metal on wood, and large areas to be printed may be filled in with felt. One block is needed for each colour in the design.

blotch: any relatively large area of uniform colour in a printed design. The printed background to the design is commonly referred to as the blotch.

burn-out print: print where a fabric containing two or more different types of fibre is printed with a substance that destroys one or more of the fibres. This results in a pattern where the printed parts of the cloth are much more open or sheer. Also known as burnt-out print, chemical print, devoré print and devourant print.

burnt-out print: *see* **burn-out print, devoré print**.

central pressure cylinder: large cylinder in a roller printing machine, around which the printing rollers are mounted. The cloth passes between the central pressure cylinder and the printing rollers.

chemical print: *see* **burn-out print, devoré print**.

colour separation: separation of the colours in a print design so that the image for each colour can be transferred to the printing machinery, eg. flat-bed screen, rotary screen, engraved roller.

colourway: one of several combinations of colours used for a particular fabric.

continuous: describes a process where the material passes in sequence through a number of stages without stopping.

converter: textile company or individual that purchases grey cloth and finishes it, including dyeing and/or printing, and then sells the finished fabric.

copper roller: heavy copper roller upon which the image to be printed is engraved for roller printing. One roller is needed for each colour in the design.

crimp print: print where areas of a cellulosic fibre fabric are printed with a thickened strong solution of caustic soda, or sodium hydroxide. The fibres contract and swell in the printed areas, leaving an excess of fabric in the unprinted areas which cockles and puckers.

devoré: descriptive of fabric that has been devoré printed.

devoré print: print where a fabric containing two or more different types of fibre is printed with a substance that destroys one or more of the fibres. This results in a pattern where the printed parts of the cloth are much more open or sheer. Also known as burn-out print, burnt-out print, chemical print and devourant print.

devourant print: *see* **devoré print, burn-out print**.

direct style: style of printing where a coloured pattern is applied to a white or lighter coloured ground. Most commonly used printing style. Note that a background dark colour or blotch can be printed.

discharge style: style of printing where a white or coloured pattern shows on a darker coloured ground. Dyed fabric is printed with a substance, the discharging agent, which removes the ground colour. The print paste may contain a colour not affected by the discharging agent giving a new colour on the cloth where it is printed.

discharge-resist process: discharge process where the colorant for the ground is applied, but not fixed, before printing the discharge paste. Fixation and discharge are subsequently achieved in a single steaming stage.

discharging agent: substance which chemically removes colour from an already dyed fabric where it is printed, leaving a white or differently coloured pattern.

doctor blade: metal blade in roller printing which removes surplus print paste from the surface of the engraved roller, leaving print paste only in the engraved areas.

duplex printing: simultaneous printing of both sides of the fabric so that the design elements coincide exactly.

dyed style: method of colouring fabric by printing with one or more mordants, fixing the mordants and dyeing the cloth with mordant dyes which only fix where the mordants have been printed.

engraved: term used in textile printing to indicate that the image for each colour in the design has been transferred to the printing machinery, eg. engraved screens, engraved copper roller.

engraved roller: describes a method of printing cloth where the image for each colour is either etched or engraved into the surface of the roller. The print paste is held in the engraved areas, and transferred to the cloth during printing.

fall-on: deliberate arrangement where one colour overlaps another colour in printing to give a third colour. Literally one colour falls on top of another colour.

P

figure: motif or prominent part of a pattern, as distinct from the ground or background.

fixation: process which effects permanent combination of the colorant with the fibre after printing and drying of the cloth. The most common method is steaming.

flat-bed screen: wood or metal frame over which is stretched a fine mesh fabric of silk, nylon, polyester or metal gauze. One screen is needed for each colour in the design, and the areas of mesh surrounding the image to be printed are blocked out so the print paste cannot penetrate.

flock: very short fibres, which may be coloured, that are used in flock printing.

flock print: print where areas of the cloth are first printed with an adhesive resin, and then very short fibres, known as flock, are applied by spraying or shaking. The flock adheres to the printed adhesive and, when dry, the surplus flock is removed. This gives a velvet-like surface, which may be enhanced by using an electrostatic charge which causes the flock to stand erect from the fabric surface. The adhesive can make the fabric stiff where printed.

flock printing: printing of an adhesive resin, onto which the flock is sprayed or shaken.

flushing: migration of dye or other chemicals leading to loss of definition in a printed fabric. This may be caused by incorrect fabric preparation, incorrect formulation of the print paste or steaming conditions that are too wet.

glitter print: print where areas of the cloth are printed with an adhesive resin, onto which glitter particles are shaken.

ground: background part of the design in a printed fabric.

half-tone: gradations of tone within one coloured area.

halo: very narrow pale band sometimes visible around all or some of the illuminating colours in a discharge or resist print. Caused by the migration of the discharging or resist agent outwards from the edges of the printed area.

hand screen printing: flat-bed screen printing where the screens are moved manually along the length of the cloth.

head colour: colorant used in the print paste when producing coloured discharge or coloured resist prints. Also known as illuminating colour.

heat transfer printing: transfer of a printed coloured design from one material (usually paper) to another (fabric) by passing the paper and fabric through heated rollers, or by using a heated press.

high pressure steaming: fixation method of steaming printed cloth where the pressure is greater than atmospheric pressure.

high temperature steaming: fixation method of steaming printed cloth where a temperature above the boiling point of water is achieved by using superheated steam.

illuminated discharge: discharge print where colour, unaffected by the discharging agent, is put into the print paste to give a new colour where printed.

illuminated resist: resist print where colour, unaffected by the resist agent, is put into the print paste to give a new colour where printed.

illuminating colour: colorant used in the print paste when producing coloured discharge or coloured resist prints. Also known as head colour.

intaglio: type of printing where the image is either etched or engraved into the printing surface, and the colorant is held in the areas below the surface.

lint doctor blade: metal blade in roller printing which removes the lint from the surface of the engraved roller. The lint is picked up by the roller from the fabric being printed.

marking-off: undesirable transfer of colour from one coloured material to another fabric.

mechanised screen printing: most flat-bed screen printing is mechanised, where the screens are fixed and the fabric moves one repeat at a time. All rotary screen printing is a continuous mechanised process, where the screens revolve and the fabric passes under them.

mélange printing: printing process where bands of colour are printed at intervals across slubbings, slivers or tops of wool or other fibres. These are subsequently steamed, washed and combed to produce a very even distribution of coloured and uncoloured lengths of fibre, where some individual fibres show colour along only part of the fibre. The effect produced in the subsequent yarn is quite different from that produced by blending dyed and undyed fibres. Also known as vigoureux printing.

mesh: material used to make a textile printing screen. Classified according to the number of holes per unit length, so finer meshes which allow more detail have a higher number.

metallic print: print where a metallic pigment has been used. Finely ground copper and aluminium alloys are mixed into a suitable binder to give gold, silver, copper and bronze effects.

migration: movement of a colorant or other added substance from one part of a textile material to another.

motif: figure or prominent part of a pattern, as distinct from the ground or background.

multicolour print: print where more than one colour is used.

one-colour print: print where one colour is used. This produces two colours on the fabric, eg. a black direct print on a white ground, a red discharge print on a black ground.

pigment: insoluble colour, which can be applied to textiles by mechanically dispersing very fine particles of the pigment in a medium, and fixing to the cloth with a suitable heat-setting resin.

pigment printing: printing using pigments, rather than dyes. The pigment is mixed into a binder containing thickener, a softener, a catalyst and a heat-setting resin. Fixation is achieved by baking to cure the resin, and no other aftertreatment is necessary.

print paste: thickened liquid used to print fabric. Print pastes for dyes contain dye, water, a thickener and other chemicals which promote dye/fibre combination.

printing: process of putting a pattern on cloth by applying colour to part of the fabric by block, engraved roller, screen or transfer.

printing styles: ways in which pattern can be achieved, eg. direct style, discharge style, resist style.

relief: type of printing where the image is in relief, or raised, on the printing machinery.

repeat: one complete unit of the textile design, containing all the elements of the design. The unit may be repeated in one of a number of ways to form the pattern on the fabric.

resist style: style of printing where a white or coloured pattern shows on a darker coloured ground. The fabric is printed with a substance that resists dye, and the fabric is then dyed. The dye fixes only where the fabric has not been printed with the resist. The print paste may contain a colour not affected by the resist that gives a new colour on the cloth where printed.

roller printing: *see* **engraved roller**.

rosin: naturally occuring resin from certain pine trees that is sometimes used as a resist in batik printing.

rotary screen: cylindrical metal mesh screen made of nickel used in rotary screen printing.

run: total length of cloth that passes through a printing machine in one batch, with no change of design or colours, eg. 10,000 metres, 200 metres.

screen printing: *see* **flat-bed screen**, **rotary screen**.

sieve: apparatus used in block printing which contains the print paste so that the even transfer of paste onto the surface of the block is facilitated.

soaping-off: aftertreatment of dyed or printed textiles with soap or a detergent to remove excess dye and other reagents.

squeegee: a straight-edged strip of rubber set into a wooden handle used to pull the print paste across the screen in flat-bed screen printing, either by hand or mechanically. In rotary screen printing the squeegee is stationary inside the rotating screen.

staining:
(1) undesirable local discolouration caused accidentally in processing or use.

(2) in colour fastness testing, the transfer of colorant from the sample being tested to adjacent materials.

(3) in textile printing, the soiling of areas of the cloth during washing-off.

steaming: fixation of dye on the printed fabric by exposing the cloth to hot, moist air. Also known as ageing.

strike-off: preliminary small-scale print to test the effectiveness of the entire printing process prior to mass production.

sublimation: process where a substance changes from a solid to a gas when heated with no intermediate liquid stage. On cooling the process reverses, ie. vapour to solid. Some disperse dyes will sublimate and can be used for transfer printing.

substrate: a material to which dyes and chemicals may be applied.

tendering: local deterioration of a fabric caused by adverse reaction between the dye or finish on the fabric and an agency such as light.

thermofixation: fixation of colorants or chemical finishes on textile materials by use of dry heat.

thermoprinting: printing of a fabric with special colorants which change their colour according to temperature.

thickener: substance used to increase the viscosity of a print paste so that it is the right consistency for printing, ie. will transfer easily from the printing machinery to the cloth, and will not spread or migrate onto the unprinted areas of the cloth. Also known as thickening agent.

thickening agent: *see* **thickener**.

transfer printing: transfer of a printed coloured design from one material (usually paper) to another (fabric), normally under the influence of heat and/or moisture and pressure. Dye transfer from the paper to the fabric occurs because the dyes are preferentially absorbed by the fibres. The process is mainly used for polyester fabrics. Most transfer printed fabric does not require a washing-off process, which is advantageous from an environmental and economic standpoint.

vigoureux printing: *see* **mélange printing**.

warp print: print where the warp yarns have been printed before the cloth is woven. When the cloth is woven, often with an undyed weft, the design shows on both sides of the cloth, with a subtle, blurred effect on the edges of the printed colours where the warp yarns have moved slightly relative to each other during weaving.

washing-off: treatment of textile in water or detergent solution to remove excess dyes or chemicals used in processing, eg. removal of surplus dyes and chemicals after fixation of the print.

wax: substance used as the mechanical resist in batik dyeing and printing.

wax print: resist print where molten wax is printed onto the cloth prior to application of the ground colour.

white pigment: extremely opaque pigment that can be printed on dark grounds. Colour can be added. The handle of the fabric is relatively stiff where printed.

Finishing

F Terms relating to finishing

anti-bacterial finish: finish which chemically inhibits bacterial growth.

anti-soil finish: finish which facilitates removal of soil or stains by ordinary domestic washing from non-absorbent, hydrophobic fibres such as polyester, and cellulosic fibre fabrics treated with durable press resins.

anti-stat finish: a starch-based finish which reduces the amount of static electricity generated by making the fabric more absorbent. Also known as anti-static finish.

anti-static finish: *see* **anti-stat finish**.

bactericide: substance which chemically inhibits bacterial growth.

beetling: treatment of damp cellulosic material, generally linen or cotton, wound onto a metal or wood beam or roller. Heavy metal or wood hammers or fallers strike the cloth with repeated blows, flattening the yarns and producing a compact, lustrous fabric.

biological attack: damage done to textiles by living plant and animal organisms.

biopolishing: treatment of cellulosic fibre fabrics with enzymes to increase the softness and smoothness of the fabric.

biostoning: enzyme treatment to give a stone-washed appearance to fabric.

biotechnology: use of living organisms or their cellular, subcellular or molecular constituents to manufacture products and establish processes.

bleaching: process of removing colour from textiles using bleaches.

bleaching agent: a chemical reagent capable of destroying partly or completely the unwanted colour in textile materials, leaving them white or considerably lighter in colour.

blowing: finishing process where moist or saturated steam is blown through a fabric, usually wool, which is generally wound on a perforated roller.

bowls: large pressure rollers between which the fabric passes in processing, eg. calendering.

brightening agent: substance that, when added to a textile material, increases the apparent brightness or whiteness by converting ultra-violet radiation into visible light. Also known as fluorescent brightening agent and optical brightening agent.

brushed fabric: term used to describe a fabric where the surface fibres or filaments have been raised to form a soft fibrous nap, eg. brushed cotton, brushed nylon.

brushing: finishing process which removes short loose fibres from the cloth.

calender: machine used in finishing consisting of a number of large pressure rollers or bowls, some of which may be heated.

calendering: finishing process where cloth in open width is passed through a series of large pressure rollers or bowls, some of which may be heated. This flattens the yarns, closes up the fabric and gives the cloth increased smoothness and lustre.

carbonising: removal of unwanted cellulosic matter, such as bits of leaf and twig, in a woollen fabric by treatment with acid. The acid destroys the cellulose but leaves the wool unharmed.

carpet beetle: species of beetle, the larvae of which attack wool and the speciality hairs.

causticising: brief treatment of cellulosic fabrics with caustic soda solution at room temperature. The fabric is held without tension, and the process increases the uptake of dyes, especially reactive dyes.

cellulase enzymes: proteins capable of degrading cellulose under optimum conditions of pH and temperature. Their use reduces fabric hairiness, leaving a softer, smoother and glossier fabric. The enzyme action weakens protruding fibres which are removed by subsequent mechanical action, and this reduces fabric pilling.

chasing calender: calender where one or more of the bowls moves faster than the others. This polishes the cloth and increases the lustre. Also known as a friction calender. Fabrics that have been finished with a chasing or friction calender are known as glazed fabrics, eg. chintz.

chemical attack: damage done to textile fibres by chemicals, eg. acids damage cellulosic fibres, and wool is damaged by alkalis.

chemical finish: finish where a substance is applied to the cloth to improve the appearance, handle or performance of the fabric.

chintz: closely woven, lustrous, plain weave cotton fabric, printed or plain, that has been friction calendered or glazed. Much used for curtainings and upholstery.

chlorination: treatment of wool with chlorine, in gaseous (dry) or liquid (wet) form, to modify the scale tips on the fibres, making smoother fibres with less capacity for felting shrinkage.

ciré: smooth woven or knitted fabric that is impregnated with a synthetic wax and passed through a friction calender. Gives a waxy or wet-look effect. Can also be achieved with heat alone on thermoplastic fibre fabrics.

cleaning: general term indicating a process which removes dirt or soil from a textile material.

clear finish: type of finish on fabrics containing wool, where the surface of the fabric is relatively free from protruding fibres, and the weave and the colours of the yarns are easily seen.

clothes moth: species of moth, the larvae of which attack wool and the speciality hairs.

controlled compressive shrinkage: finishing process where the fabric is pre-shrunk to specific dimensions by a combination of heat, moisture and pressure, forcing the compressed fabric to shrink in length. Reduces relaxation and swelling shrinkage in cotton. Trade names include Sanforized and Rigmel.

converter: textile company or individual that purchases grey cloth and finishes it, including dyeing and/or printing, and then sells the finished fabric. Usually, but not always, the converter does not own machinery, and the processing is done by a commission dyer/finisher.

crabbing: process used for worsted fabrics to set them in a smooth flat state so that they will not distort during subsequent wet processing. Essentially the fabric is stabilised by treating the fabric under warp-wise tension in hot or boiling water and allowing it to cool while still under tension.

crease-resist finish: wet finish applied to fabrics which crease to improve their resistance to and recovery from creasing.

crease-resist resin: reagent used in finishing on fabrics which crease to improve their resistance to and recovery from creasing.

creasing: formation of unwanted folds and puckers in fabric during use, which adversely affect the appearance.

crêpe: fabric where the crêpe effect is produced in finishing by treatment with embossing rollers, engraved with a crêpe pattern, which impart a crêpe effect onto the fabric through heat and pressure.

crêping: wet finishing treatment for crêpe fabrics where the yarns are allowed to relax into a twist-lively state. This develops the characteristic crinkled or puckered surface.

cropping: finishing process where the surface fibres on a fabric are cut level. Also known as shearing and cutting.

curing: heat treatment, at a specified temperature, of a reagent applied to a fabric or garment during finishing. The heat effects a chemical reaction between the textile and the previously applied reagent, eg. a crease-resist resin.

cutting: finishing process where the surface fibres on a fabric are cut level. Also known as cropping and shearing.

cuttling: process of either folding finished fabric down the middle and placing in folds of predetermined length, or placing open width fabric in loose transverse folds.

decatising: finishing process used on fabrics containing wool, where dry steam is blown through the fabric to improve the handle and appearance.

desizing: removal from the fabric of size or starches put on the warp yarns to strengthen them for the strains of weaving.

detergent: substance, usually having surface-active properties, specifically used for cleansing.

dimensional stability: ability of a textile to retain its size and shape through processing and use.

distressed: describes fabric which has been deliberately aged in appearance by a finishing process, eg. bleaching, stone-washing.

dress-face finish: finish for wool fabrics where milling, raising and cropping produce a fabric with a soft lustrous nap, eg. doeskin.

drip-dry: describes fabrics where crease resistance is good during wear and washing, and minimum ironing is necessary to maintain a good appearance.

dry finish: finish which involves physical treatment of the cloth without the use of water by a machine to produce the desired effect. Also known as mechanical finish and physical finish.

durable: describes any finish reasonably resistant to normal usage, washing and/or dry-cleaning.

durable press: finishing treatment with heat and resin, or heat alone, which gives the fabric or garment a specific shape which will be retained through normal usage, washing and/or dry-cleaning.

easy-care: describes fabrics where crease resistance is good during wear and washing, and minimum ironing is necessary to maintain a good appearance.

embossed crêpe: fabric with a crêpe appearance achieved by rollers, engraved with a crêpe pattern, on an embossing calender.

embossing: production of a relief pattern on a fabric by passing it through an embossing calender, where one of the heated metal bowls is engraved with a pattern.

embossing calender: calender where one of the heated metal bowls is engraved with a pattern. The pattern is pressed onto the cloth as it moves through the calender.

emerizing: finishing process where the fabric is passed over a series of emery-covered rollers to produce a suede-like finish.

enzyme: one of a number of naturally occurring complex proteins that acts as a catalyst in biochemical reactions.

FBA: *see* **fluorescent brightening agent**.

felting shrinkage: shrinkage of wool and other animal hair fibres due mainly to the scale structure on the fibre surface. Can be reduced by modification of the fibre surface to make it smoother.

fibrillation: formation of a fine network of interconnected fibres, where the fine fibrils so produced partially peel away from the fibre surface. Used in finishing lyocell fabrics to develop their characteristic handle and drape.

finish: process, physical or chemical, that is applied to a textile to improve the appearance, handle or performance.

finishing: processing, physical or chemical, of textile material that improves the appearance, handle or performance.

fire resistant: describes a textile with a chemical finish which will suppress, significantly reduce or delay combustion of the material. Also known as fire retardant.

fire retardant: describes a textile with a chemical finish which will suppress, significantly reduce or delay combustion of the material. Also known as fire resistant.

flame resistance: property of a material, either inherent or because a suitable finish has been applied, whereby flaming combustion is slowed, terminated or prevented.

flame resistant: describes a textile with a chemical finish whereby flaming combustion is slowed, terminated or prevented. Sometimes the flame resistance is achieved by modification of the fibre during fibre manufacture. Also known as flame retardant.

flame retardant: describes a textile with a chemical finish whereby flaming combustion is slowed, terminated or prevented. Sometimes the flame retardance is achieved by modification of the fibre during fibre manufacture. Also known as flame resistant.

flammability: ability of a textile to burn with a flame under specified test conditions

fluorescent brightening agent: substance that, when added to a textile material, increases the apparent brightness or whiteness by converting ultra-violet radiation into visible light. Also known as brightening agent and optical brightening agent.

friction calender: calender where one or more of the bowls moves faster than the others. This polishes the cloth and increases the lustre. Also known as a chasing calender. Fabrics that have been finished with a chasing or friction calender are known as glazed fabrics, eg. chintz.

fulling: finishing process where the fabric is consolidated or compacted by a combination of heat, moisture and mechanical pressure. Utilises the ability of wool and other animal hairs to felt. Also known as milling.

fungi: plant forms which have no chlorophyll and derive nourishment from organic matter. Examples include moulds and mildews.

fungicides: substances that destroy fungi.

glazed fabric: fabric with a smooth, glossy surface produced by friction calendering, with or without additional substances, such as starch or a synthetic resin, applied to the fabric before calendering.

glazing: process of producing a glazed fabric by friction calendering.

F

greige cloth: cloth before it has been bleached, dyed or finished. Also known as grey cloth.

grey cloth: cloth before it has been bleached, dyed or finished. Also known as greige cloth.

heat setting: process of treating a textile, in fibre, yarn, fabric or garment form, with heat followed by cooling to give the textile dimensional stability. With thermoplastic fibres the effect is permanent, provided that the temperature of heat setting is not approached in subsequent processing or use.

loomstate cloth: woven cloth after removal from the loom and before it has been finished.

mangle: machine consisting of two or more rollers or bowls running in contact to form a nip (or nips), the purpose of which is to remove excess liquid from textiles which are passed through it.

mechanical finish: finish which involves physical treatment of the cloth by a machine to produce the desired effect. Also known as dry finish and physical finish.

mercerisation: process of treating cotton and linen yarns and fabrics with a solution of caustic alkali, generally caustic soda, which is sodium hydroxide. The fibres are swollen, and the strength and dye affinity are increased. The textile is generally held under tension to increase the lustre.

microporous polymer laminate: continuous membrane with extremely small pores or holes, which are big enough to allow the passage of water vapour, but are too small to allow water droplets to penetrate. Trade names include Goretex.

mildew: a growth of certain species of minute fungi, which flourish in damp, warm conditions.

milling: finishing process where the fabric is consolidated or compacted by a combination of heat, moisture and mechanical pressure. Utilises the property of wool and other animal hairs to felt, owing to the overlapping scale structure on the fibre surface. Also known as fulling.

moiré:
(1) finish where a wavy watermark pattern is produced by calendering, usually on a fabric showing a rib or cord effect in the weft direction. The moiré effect can be produced either by embossing with a roller engraved with a moiré pattern, or by feeding two layers of fabric face to face through the calender. The effect may be permanent or temporary depending on the fibre(s) and chemicals used.
(2) fabric which shows a moiré pattern.

moth damage: damage inflicted on wool and other animal hair fibres by the larvae of the clothes moth.

mothproof finish: finish which makes the fibre unpalatable to the larvae or grubs which hatch out from the eggs laid by the moth.

mould / mold: a growth of certain species of minute fungi, which flourish in damp, warm conditions.

nap: soft fibrous surface produced on a fabric by raising; a finishing process where some of the fibres are lifted from the fabric surface.

napping: finishing process where some of the fibres are lifted from the surface of the cloth by rollers covered with fine flexible wire teeth to form a soft fibrous surface called a nap. Also known as raising.

nip: point of contact between two rollers or bowls.

OBA: *see* **optical brightening agent**.

oil cloth: cotton fabric that has been treated on one side with a drying oil to make it impervious to water.

oil-based liquid: liquid where an oil or fat is a large component, eg. salad dressing, gravy.

oiled silk: silk fabric made impervious to water by treatment with a drying oil.

oilskin: fabric which has been rendered impervious to water by treatment with a drying oil such as linseed.

optical brightening agent: substance that, when added to a textile material, increases the apparent brightness or whiteness by converting ultra-violet radiation into visible light. Also known as brightening agent and fluorescent brightening agent.

pad mangle: type of mangle for impregnating fabric in open width with a liquor or paste, as the fabric is passed through one or more nips.

padding mangle: *see* **pad mangle**.

padding: process of impregnating a fabric with a liquor or paste, by passing through a padding mangle.

perforated beam: beam or roller with holes through which dye-liquor or steam can be passed. The fabric to be treated is wound onto the roller.

permanent: describes a finish where the effect produced by the finish does not alter or change until the fabric disintegrates.

permanent creases: intended permanent creases put into a garment, eg. knife-edge creases in trousers.

permanent pleats: pleats put into a fabric or garment by a method, usually involving heat, which ensures the pleats will remain through subsequent use and aftercare.

permanent press: finishing treatment which gives the fabric or garment a specific shape which will be retained through normal usage, washing and/or dry-cleaning.

permanent set: treatment of textile in fibre, yarn, fabric or garment form to ensure permanent dimensional stability.

physical finish: finish which involves physical treatment of the cloth by a machine to produce the desired effect. Also known as dry finish and mechanical finish.

polymer resin: substance used in a finishing treatment to produce a particular durable effect, eg. glazing of a cotton fabric, permanent press on non-thermoplastic fibres such as viscose.

post-cure: describes a process where a fabric is impregnated with a resin, and the resin is cured after the garment is made.

pre-cure: describes a process where a fabric is impregnated with a resin, and the resin is partially cured before the garment is made.

pre-shrunk: describes a textile material that has been shrunk in finishing to predetermined dimensions to minimise shrinkage in use and aftercare.

pressing: application of pressure, with or without steaming or heating, to remove unintended creases and smooth fabrics and garments. Also used to introduce desired creases in garments.

proof: fully resistant to a specified agency, ie. total resistance to the agent can be shown by standardised tests.

raising: finishing process where some of the fibres are lifted from the surface of the cloth by rollers covered with fine flexible wire teeth to form a soft fibrous surface called a nap. Also known as napping.

relaxation shrinkage: shrinkage occurring when the stretching caused by stresses and strains imposed on the fibres and yarns during processing and fabric manufacture disappears under wet or damp conditions when the fabric is not held.

repellent: describes a degree of resistance to a particular agency, eg. water repellent.

resin: substance used in a wet finishing treatment to give a particular property to a fabric, eg. durable press.

resistant: describes a degree of resistance to a particular agency, eg. crease resistant.

retardant: describes a degree of resistance to a particular agency, eg. flame retardant.

rigging: lengthways folding of fabric so that the folded fabric is half its original width.

rinsing: treatment with clean water to remove unwanted matter, such as surplus chemicals.

rot-resist finish: finish which prevents rotting or natural decay.

sand-washed: term used to describe silk or manufactured fibre fabric finished to give a peach-skin appearance and handle. Originally achieved by gentle abrasion with a sand and water mixture, and now generally done by washing with detergents and enzymes rather than sand. Also *see* **washed silk** and **emerizing**.

schreinered fabric: fabric that has been passed through a schreiner calender to increase the lustre.

schreinering: calendering using a schreiner calender where one metal bowl is engraved with very fine slanting parallel lines. This gives the fabric increased lustre.

scouring: washing treatment of a textile to remove natural fats and waxes, dirt, oil and other impurities.

semi-durable: describes a finish that will last through several launderings or dry-cleanings.

shearing:
(1) finishing process where the surface fibres on a fabric are cut level. Also known as cropping and cutting.
(2) cutting loose fibres or yarn from the surface of a fabric after weaving.

shrinkage: reduction in length and/or width of a textile caused by processing or after-care.

shrink-resist: describes a textile material that is dimensionally stable.

shrink-resist finish: finish, which may be physical or chemical, that gives a fabric improved dimensional stability.

singeing: preparatory finishing process where unwanted fibres protruding from the surface of the cloth are removed by passing the fabric very quickly over either an open flame or very hot metal plates.

size: substances put onto warp yarns to strengthen and lubricate them for the strains of weaving.

slack mercerisation: mercerisation of a cellulosic fabric without tension or under reduced tension. The process improves the stretch properties of the fabric. Dye absorption is increased but the lustre remains unchanged.

soap: salt of a long chain fatty acid, that has detergent properties.

softener: *see* **softening agent**.

softening agent: substance added to a textile in finishing to give a softer handle, eg. oils, fats and waxes. Also known as softener.

soil release finish: finish put onto certain fabrics which soil easily, eg. polyester, cellulosics treated with a durable press resin. Water absorbency is improved and formation of static electricity is reduced.

solvent scour: cleaning treatment of a textile in an organic solvent.

stain: undesirable local discolouration caused accidentally in processing or use, eg. ink spilt on a carpet, gravy splashed on a tablecloth.

stain repellent finish: finish which inhibits the absorption of water-based and oil-based liquids. Trade names include Teflon.

starch: carbohydrate component extracted from certain plants and used for sizing yarns in weaving, and in finishing to improve the appearance and handle of certain fabrics.

static electricity: electricity produced by materials rubbing together. Can be a problem with synthetic fibres with low absorbency. Solved by building in anti-stat properties during fibre manufacture, or by applying an anti-stat, starch-based finish.

steaming: treatment with steam to achieve a variety of results in finishing, eg. blowing steam through wool fabric tightly wound onto a perforated beam improves the lustre.

stenter: machine with moving endless bands of either pins or clips which hold the selvedges and carry the fabric in open width through a hot air cabinet. The machine is used for drying, heat-setting, controlling fabric width and other finishing processes.

stentering: process of passing a fabric through the stenter.

stone-washing: treatment where fabrics or garments are deliberately aged or distressed by the mechanical action of either pebbles, pumice stones or other abradants during washing.

sueded fabric: fabric finished to give a suede-like appearance, often achieved by using emery-covered rollers. Also *see* **emerizing**.

sueding: finishing process which gives the fabric the appearance of suede leather. Also *see* **emerizing**.

surface wetting: making the surface of the cloth wet, eg. drops of rain on a cotton jacket.

surfactant: agent, soluble or dispersible in a liquid, which decreases the surface tension of the liquid. It is a contraction of the term *surface-active agent*, and examples include soaps and detergents.

swelling shrinkage: shrinkage where the fibres absorb water, swell and become shorter, causing the fabric to shrink.

temporary: describes a finish which substantially disappears with the first washing or dry-cleaning.

tenter: machine for drying wool fabrics, similar to a stenter.

tentering: process of passing a wool fabric through the tenter.

warp starches: carbohydrate substances which are the main constituent of size.

wash and wear: describes fabrics and garments where crease resistance is good during wear and washing, and minimum or no ironing is necessary to maintain a good appearance.

washed silk: silk fabric slightly abraded in finishing to increase the softness and subdue the lustre. *See* **emerizing**.

water repellency: relative resistance of a fabric to surface wetting, water penetration and water absorption.

water repellent: describes a fabric that resists surface wetting, water penetration and water absorption, but allows the passage of air and water vapour.

water repellent finish: finish on a fabric which improves the resistance of the fabric to surface wetting, water penetration and water absorption, but allows the passage of air and water vapour.

water-based liquid: liquid where water is a large component, eg. coffee, fruit juice.

watered: descriptive term for fabric showing a moiré effect, derived from the characteristic wavy watermark pattern.

waterproof: describes a fabric or finish where there is total resistance to penetration by water, eg. PVC-coated cotton, rubberised fabric.

wet finish: any finishing process where the fabric is treated with a liquid, usually water. The term covers both chemical finishing, where added substances improve the appearance, handle or performance of the fabric, and other wet finishing processes such as scouring and rinsing.

Appendix

Trade names and abbreviations

Notes to the Appendix

Trade names

All trade names are listed alphabetically.

eg. **Comex**
Coolmax
Cordura

The name of the manufacturing company is in italics.

eg. *Courtaulds*

Any list of trade names is necessarily out of date as soon as it is published. As far as was possible the information was checked before going to press: the authors would welcome updates as and where necessary, and thank all who helped to ensure accuracy for this edition. New products come on the market constantly, and existing products are withdrawn. It is therefore recommended that the reader checks with the manufacturing company.

Abbreviations

Abbreviations are listed alphabetically in Tables A and B.

Trade names

TRADE NAME	PRODUCT DESCRIPTION	COMPANY
Actifresh	antibacterial and antifungal reagent	*British Sanitized*
Actigard	antimicrobial reagent	*Sanitized Marketing*
Aerotex 3000	fabrics used for headrests and pillow covers on public transport	
Aflamman AH	flame retardant	*Thor Chemicals*
Alcantara	synthetic suede-look fabrics marketed in Italy under this name	*Toray*
Amgard	flame retardant	*Albright & Wilson*
Amicor	antibacterial acrylic fibre for apparel	*Courtaulds*
Amicor Plus	antifungal and antibacterial acrylic fibre for apparel	*Courtaulds*
ANSO	polyamide fibre for carpets	*Allied Signal Carpet Fibres*
Antron	polyamide fibre for carpets	*DuPont*
Antron Excel	polyamide textured yarn for carpets	*DuPont*
Antron Stainmaster	polyamide fibre for carpets	*DuPont*
Aquatex	range of specialist high performance fabrics incorporating a breathable waterproof membrane **Porelle**	*Porvair plc*
Arnel	triacetate	*Celanese USA*
Axtar	polyester filament nonwoven fabric	
Bilorex	nylon and elastomeric yarn	*Wykes of Leicester*
Biokryl	antibacterial acrylic fibre for technical end uses	*Courtaulds*

TRADE NAME	PRODUCT DESCRIPTION	COMPANY
Biokryl Plus	antifungal and antibacterial acrylic fibre for technical end uses	*Courtaulds*
Biosoft PW	enzyme treatment for wool	*Nova Nordisk and T S Chemicals*
Breathe	microporous polyurethane membrane	*UCB Speciality Chemicals Division*
Cambrelle	range of nonwoven fabrics largely used for shoe linings	*DuPont*
Cashmeera	polyester shingosen fabric	*Toyobo*
Cashmilon	acrylic	*Asahi*
Celanese	acetate	*Celanese USA*
Centran	high modulus polyethylene fibre	*Celanese USA*
Comex	aramid	*Teijin*
Coolmax	polyester with good humidity transfer used for active sportswear	*DuPont*
Cordura	range of polyamide fibres used for fabrics for luggage and backpacks	*DuPont*
Coro	air textured polyamide yarn	*Nylstar*
Courtaulds Lyocell	HT solvent spun cellulosic fibre for technical applications	*Courtaulds*
Courtelle	acrylic	*Courtaulds*
Courtelle Fusion	mixture shade range of acrylic fibre	*Courtaulds*
Courtelle LC	speciality bicomponent acrylic with a soft handle	*Courtaulds*
Courtelle Supermatt	acrylic fibre with matt appearance and very soft handle	*Courtaulds*
Couru	range of fabrics containing 75% wool/25% **Tactel** polyamide microfibre	*OMC (Carrington Viyella)*

TRADE NAME	PRODUCT DESCRIPTION	COMPANY
Cyclone	waterproof, windproof breathable high performance fabrics	*Carrington Performance Fabrics*
Cygnet	breathable waterproof membrane	
Dacron	polyester fibre	*DuPont*
Dacron Comforel	tiny balls of polyester fibre used for duvets on feather and down duvet filling machines	*DuPont*
Dacron Hollofil	polyester made for filling duvets and sleeping bags	*DuPont*
Dacron Quallofil 7	polyester made for filling duvets and sleeping bags	*DuPont*
Danaklon Hy-Colour	spun-dyed polypropylene yarn	*Danaklon*
Danaklon Hy-Dry	hydrophilic polypropylene yarn	*Danaklon*
Danaklon Hy-Speed	polypropylene yarn	*Danaklon*
Danaklan Hy-Strength	polypropylene yarn	*Danaklon*
Danufil	standard and modified viscose staple for a variety of end uses	*Courtaulds*
Decora	spun-dyed polyester yarn	*Rhone Poulenc*
Delicana	antibacterial odour-free polyamide	*Toray*
Dicel	acetate	*Novaceta*
Dicelesta	acetate/polyester blended yarn	*Novaceta*
Dinkan	fabric with ultra moisture permeability	*Unitika*
Diolen	polyester high tenacity yarn	*Akzo Nobel*
Diolen	polyester yarn Variations include **Diolen, Diolen Linetex, Diolen Crinkle** and **Sedura**	*Kuagtextil*
Diolen 174 SLC	high tenacity polyester yarn for coated fabrics	*Akzo Nobel*
Dolanit	acrylic	*Courtaulds*

TRADE NAME	PRODUCT DESCRIPTION	COMPANY
Dolan	acrylic	*Courtaulds*
Dorlastan	elastane	*Bayer*
Dralon	acrylic	*Bayer*
Dralon Micro Fibre	acrylic microfibre	*Bayer*
Dunova	acrylic	*Bayer*
Dyneema	extremely strong polyethylene fibre for technical textiles	*DSM High Performance Fibres*
Ecospun	hollow siliconised conjugate (spiral crimp) polyester fibre made from recycled polyester	
Emera Windliner	windproof breathable membrane	*Akzo Nobel*
Enka Sun	continuous filament viscose with inbuilt UV (ultra-violet) protector	*Akzo Nobel*
Enka Viscose	continuous filament viscose The Viscose Circle of Quality gold card label ensures quality through all stages of production	*Akzo Nobel*
Enkalon	nylon (polyamide) high tenacity filament yarn	*Akzo Nobel*
Entrant	high performance waterproof fabric with moisture-permeable inner surface	*Toray*
Escain	synthetic suede-look fabrics marketed in Japan	*Toray*
Esmo	polyester fibres impregnated with minute inorganic particles which shield the wearer from UV (ultra-violet) rays and reflect solar heat	*Kuraray*
Eural	polyester/wool blend using **Tergal**	*Rhone Poulenc*
Evlan	coarse denier viscose staple	*Courtaulds*
Expel	fabric treated with insect repellent	*Graniteville USA*
Fibravyl	chlorofibre	*Rhovyl*
Fibro	viscose staple	*Courtaulds*

TRADE NAME	PRODUCT DESCRIPTION	COMPANY
Fibro H	viscose for nonwovens	Courtaulds
Fidion	polyester	Montefibre
Fidion FR	flame retardant polyester	Montefibre
Flammentin FMB	flame retardant	Thor Chemicals
Fortrel	polyester	Wellman International
Geena	polyester filament fabric	Toyobo
Goretex	breathable waterproof fabric where a continuous membrane with extremely small pores or holes is combined with one or more textile components	W L Gore & Associates
Hydroflect MVP	breathable hydrophilic coating	
Inidex	flame retardant modified acrylic	Courtaulds
Karecaron	modacrylic developed by and marketed exclusively in Europe by Variations include **Kanecaron Protex M** and **Kanecaron SYS**	Kaneka Corporation Waxman International
Kermel	aramid	Rhone Poulenc
Kevlar	high tenacity aramid fibre	DuPont
Leacril	acrylic	Montefibre
Leacril HT	acrylic fibre for outdoor applications	Montefibre
Leacril Micro	acrylic microfibre	Montefibre
Lenzing Lyocell	lyocell	Lenzing
Lenzing Modal	modal	Lenzing
Lenzing Modal Micro	modal microfibre	Lenzing
Lenzing Viscose FR	flame retardant viscose	Lenzing
Lenzing Viscose SC	crimped viscose	Lenzing

TRADE NAME	PRODUCT DESCRIPTION	COMPANY
Lenzing Viscose TC	viscose with star-shaped cross section	*Lenzing*
Lilion	polyamide	*Snia Fibre*
Linel	elastane fibre	*Fillaticce SpA*
Lurex	metallic yarn	*The Lurex Co Ltd*
Lycra	elastane fibre	*DuPont*
Lycra Soft	trademark for fabrics and garments made from Lycra Type 902 C	*DuPont*
Meraklon	polypropylene fibre	*Moplefan* (*Montedison* and *Hercules*)
Meryl	polyamide	*Nylstar*
Meryl Micro	polyamide microfibre	*Nylstar*
Micrell	polyester continuous filament microfibre	*Noyfil and Val Lesina*
Micromattique	polyester microfibre	*DuPont*
Micro Safe AM	antimicrobial acetate	*Trevira USA*
Microban	antimicrobial additive	
Microfibre Dralon	acrylic microfibre	*Bayer*
Microlene	polypropylene fibre	*Polymekon*
Microsupplex	polyamide microfibre	*DuPont*
Miracosmo	polyamide	*Toray*
Multi	polyamide microfibre	*Nylstar*
Myflam	flame retardant	*Mydrin*
Myoliss	acrylic microfibre	*Montefibre*
Mytex	flame resistant coating	*Mydrin*
Neochrome	producer-dyed acrylic	*Courtaulds*
Neoprene	synthetic rubber	
Neulana	shrink resistance and machine washability treatment for wool	*Woolcombers Processors Limited*

TRADE NAME	PRODUCT DESCRIPTION	COMPANY
Newcell	lyocell filament	*Courtaulds* and *Akzo Nobel*
Nomex	aramid fibre with high temperature resistance used for fire-fighting clothing	*DuPont*
Noval	range of polyamide fibres and yarns for carpets and technical textile applications	*Novalis*
Novalene	acetate multifilament bright yarn	*Novaceta*
Oasis	highly absorbent polyacrylate	*Courtaulds* and *Allied Colloids*
PBI	flame and chemical resistant fibre	*Hoechst Trevira*
Permatex	waterproof, windproof, hydrophilic, breathable polyurethane membrane	*J B Broadley*
Polartec	trade name for polyester fleece high performance fabrics, some of which use a percentage of polyester recycled from plastic bottles Types currently available include **Polartec 100**, **Polartec 200, Polartec 300**, **Polartec Micro, Polartec Power Stretch, Polartec Windblock, Polartec Thermal Stretch** and **Polartec XT**	*Malden Mills*
Poliloft	polyester filament dyeable at ordinary temperature and pressure	*Toray*
Polysorb	hydrophilic polyester fibre	*Wellman International*
Pontella	polyester with octolobal cross section	*Rhone Poulenc*
Porelle	windproof, waterproof breathable membrane Variations include **Porelle 55** and **Porelle IV**	*Porvair plc*
Proban	flame retardant	*Albright & Wilson*

TRADE NAME	PRODUCT DESCRIPTION	COMPANY
Proofae	polyurethane membrane where a ceramic layer is applied to give micropores, producing a windproof, waterproof breathable membrane	
Pyrovatex	flame retardant	Ciby Geigy
Pyrovatex CP	flame retardant	Ciby Geigy
Reemay	nonwoven filament polyester fabric	Reemay Inc
Retravyl	chlorofibre	Rhovyl
Rhonel	polyamide	Rhone Poulenc
Rhonel Satine	fine, lustrous, polyamide hosiery yarn	Nylstar
Rhonel Sylkharesse	opaque polyamide hosiery yarn with a soft handle	Nylstar
Rhovyl	chlorofibre	Rhovyl
Rigmel	trade name for a controlled compressive shrinkage process	Bradford Dyeing Association
Roica	elastane products	Asahi
Sanforized	trade name for a controlled compressive shrinkage process	Cluett Peabody & Co Inc
Sarille	medium denier viscose staple	Courtaulds
Scotchguard	fluorochemical stain repellent	3M Chemicals Group
Setila	polyester fine filament yarn	Rhone Poulenc
Setila Micro	polyester microfilament yarn	Rhone Poulenc
Setila Soft	polyester filament yarn	Rhone Poulenc
Silcolour	spun-dyed bright acetate filament yarn	Novaceta
Sildull	spun-dyed matt acetate filament yarn	Novaceta
Silene	acetate filament yarn	Novaceta
Silfresh	antimicrobial acetate yarn	Novaceta
Silnova	acetate multifilament matt yarn	Novaceta
Sironil	acrylic	Enimont

TRADE NAME	PRODUCT DESCRIPTION	COMPANY
Situssa	acetate/polyamide blended yarn	*Novaceta*
Socio	polyester shingosen fabric	*Toyobo*
Solar-Alfa	fabric made from **Thermatron** yarns which contain zirconium carbide They abstract warmth from sunlight and near infra-red and emit far infra-red	
Sontara	spunlaced nonwoven fabric	*DuPont*
Souple Antistatic	polyamide with antistatic properties	*Nylstar*
Stera-tex	waterproof, breathable protective fabric	*Aquatex Functional Fabrics*
Stomatex NE	microthermal fabric made from **Neoprene**	*Micro Thermal Systems Ltd*
Styl	polyamide	*Snia Fibre*
Sun-Select	range of tan-through fabrics, where the fabric is claimed to block out the harmful UV-B rays of the sun, while allowing the UV-A rays to reach the skin and safely tan it	*Interlad*
Superwash	trade name for a shrink-resist process for wool, which combines chlorination of the fibres with addition of a polymer resin	
Supplex	polyamide fibre	*DuPont*
Sway	fabric which changes colour with fluctuations in temperature	*Toray*
Sympatex	waterproof, windproof, breathable, hydrophilic polyester membrane	*Akzo Nobel*
Tactel	polyamide fibre	*DuPont*
Tactel Aquator	range of two-layer high performance/ high comfort fabrics using polyamide in conjunction with a cotton or other fibre layer	*DuPont*
Tactel diablo	polyamide fibre with novel cross section	*DuPont*

TRADE NAME	PRODUCT DESCRIPTION	COMPANY
Tactel micro	polyamide microfibre	*DuPont*
Tactel microtouch	polyamide microfibre	*DuPont*
Tactel Multisoft	polyamide with fine filament	*DuPont*
Tactel Strata	polyamide with bitonal effect	*DuPont*
Tactesse	polyamide for carpets	
Tana lawn	range of printed and plain fine cotton lawn fabrics exclusive to Liberty	*Liberty*
Technora	aramid	*Teijin*
Teflon	PTFE stain, soil and water repellent	*DuPont*
Tekton	polypropylene fibre	*Reemay Inc*
Telar	apparel yarn composed mainly of polypropylene	*Filament Fibre Technology Inc*
Tencel	staple and filament lyocell for apparel	*Courtaulds*
Tendrelle	polyamide	
Tergal	polyester	*Rhone Poulenc*
Terinda	polyester fibre	*DuPont*
Terital	polyester	*Montefibre*
Terital Fine Denier	polyester continuous filament microfibre	*Montefibre*
Terital Microspun	polyester staple microfibre	*Montefibre*
Terital TBM	thermal bonding polyester fibre	*Montefibre*
Terital Zero 4	polyester continuous filament microfibre	*Montefibre*
Tetoron	polyester	*Teijin*
Thermastat	fabrics for thermal wear made from hollow polyester which provide warmth, moisture control and comfort quality controlled by	*DuPont*
Thermatron	high performance yarn containing zirconium carbide	
Thermax	hollow polyester fibre	*DuPont*

TRADE NAME	PRODUCT DESCRIPTION	COMPANY
Thermolite	polyester staple	*DuPont*
Thermoloft	polyester staple (high performance)	*DuPont*
Toraysee	microfibre fabric used as cleaning cloth for spectacles	*Toray*
Trevira	polyester	*Hoechst Trevira*
Trevira 350	low-pill polyester staple fibre	*Hoechst Trevira*
Trevira 353	low-pill polyester staple fibre	*Hoechst Trevira*
Trevira CS	flame retardant polyester	*Hoechst Trevira*
Trevira Finesse	polyester microfibre	*Hoechst Trevira*
Trevira Fleece	polyester thermal fabric	*Hoechst Trevira*
Trevira High Tenacity	high strength polyester	*Hoechst*
Trevira Micronesse	polyester microfibre	*Hoechst Trevira*
Trevira Two	a mixture of virgin polyester and polyester recycled from plastic bottles	*Trevira USA*
Triad	waterproof, windproof breathable membrane	
TTP	textile tow precursor acrylic fibre for manufacture of carbon fibre	*Courtaulds*
Twaron	aramid	*Akzo Nobel*
Twaron CT	continuous filament aramid microfibre used for bullet-proof vests	*Akzo Nobel*
Tygasil	woven ceramic fabric	
Tyglas	woven glass fabric	
Typar	spunbonded polypropylene backing nonwoven fabric	*DuPont*
Tyvek	spunbonded polyethylene nonwoven fabric	*DuPont*
Ultrasuede	synthetic suede-look fabrics marketed in the USA under this name	*Toray*
Varuna	range of printed and plain fine wool challis fabrics exclusive to Liberty	*Liberty*

TRADE NAME	PRODUCT DESCRIPTION	COMPANY
Vectran	liquid crystal polymer	*Trevira USA*
Velicren FR	flame retardant modacrylic	*Montefibre*
Vent-A-Layer	range of high performance clothing	*Dawson Consumer Products*
Viloft	viscose modified staple for special end uses Variations include **Viloft Cascade**, **Viloft Excel**, **Viloft Finesse**, **Viloft Original** and **Viloft Ultrafine**	*Courtaulds*
Visil	flame resistant viscose fibre containing polysilic acid	*Kemira Fibres*
Vivrelle	polyoxamide	*Snia Fibre*
Viyella	range of fabrics using lambswool and/or cotton, sometimes blended with polyester. Typical fibre compositions include 100% cotton, 100% lambswool, and 45% cotton/ 55% lambswool	*Coats Viyella plc*
Vonnel	acrylic	*FISIPE SA*
Wellblend	thermal bonding polyester fibre	*Wellman International*
Wistel TM	spun-dyed polyester filament	*Snia Fibre*
XCR	Extended Comfort Range ultralight windproof waterproof lining	*W L Gore & Associates*
Zirpo	flame retardant treatment for wool	

Abbreviations

Table A **Codes for generic man-made fibre names**

ALG	alginate
AR	aramid
CA	acetate
CF	carbon
CLF	chlorofibre
CLY	lyocell
CMD	modal
CUP	cupro
CV	viscose
CTA	triacetate
ED	elastodiene
EL	elastane
GF	glass
MAC	modacrylic
MTF	metal
PA	polyamide
PAN	acrylic
PE	polyethylene
PES	polyester
PI	polyimide
POA	polyoxyamide
PP	polypropylene
PTFE	fluorofibre
PVAL	vinylal

Source: BISFA - The International Bureau for the Standardisation of Man-Made Fibres.
NB. This coding is due to be recognised as an ISO standard by the end of 1997.

Table B **Codes for generic natural fibre names and other commonly found abbreviations**

BCF	bulked continuous filament
CAD	computer aided design
CAM	computer aided manufacture
CIM	computer integrated manufacture and management
CO	cotton
FBA	fluorescent brightening agent
FCS	flat cross section
FR	flame retardant
HM	high modulus
HT	high tenacity/ high temperature
KDK	knit-de-knit
LI	linen or flax
ML	multilobal
OBA	optical brightening agent
PVA	polyvinyl alcohol
PVC	polyvinyl chloride
PVDC	polyvinylidene chloride
SI	silk
WO	wool